Born To Win!

Success Strategies for Young Businesses and New Entrepreneurs

by

Jennifer McLeod

Bloomington, IN  Milton Keynes, UK

AuthorHouse™
1663 Liberty Drive, Suite 200
Bloomington, IN 47403
www.authorhouse.com
Phone: 1-800-839-8640

AuthorHouse™ UK Ltd.
500 Avebury Boulevard
Central Milton Keynes, MK9 2BE
www.authorhouse.co.uk
Phone: 08001974150

© 2006 Jennifer McLeod. All rights reserved.

No part of this book may be reproduced, stored in a retrieval system, or transmitted by any means without the written permission of the author.

First published by AuthorHouse 7/19/2006
ISBN: 1-4259-2391-7 (sc)

Printed in the United States of America
Bloomington, Indiana

This book is printed on acid-free paper.

All rights reserved. No part of this book may be reproduced by any mechanical, photographic, or electronic process, or in the form of photographic recording, nor may it be stored in a retrieval system, transmitted, or otherwise be copied for public or private use without prior written permission of the publisher.

The rights of Jennifer McLeod as author of this work have been asserted in accordance with the Copyright, Designs and Patents Act 1988.

The intent of the author is only to offer information of a general nature to help you in your quest for success and enlightenment. In the event that you use any of the information in this book for yourself, the author and the publisher assume no responsibility of your actions.

Dedication

I dedicate this book to my two children Ricardo and Nathaniel that it may inspire them to go forward and be the leaders that they are destined to be.

Jennifer

Table of Contents

Dedication v

Acknowledgements..ix

Introduction..xi

Chapter 1 – The Power of Belief............................ 1

Chapter 2 – How To Develop A Better Relationship With Yourself 31

Chapter 3 – How To Get Rid Of Fear And Get On With Your Business And Your Life 53

Chapter 4 – Secrets Of Dynamic Goal Achievement That Will Take You To The Stars And Beyond. 75

Chapter 5 – How To Energise Your Mind, Body And Spirit... 87

Chapter 6 – Secrets Of The Entrepreneur's Dream 101

How Jennifer McLeod Can Help You Further 135

Share Your Success Story 137

Acknowledgements

My sincere thanks and appreciation goes to Ewemade (Maddy) Orobator of Grow and Prosper Ltd. His unconditional support and words of wisdom at the early stages of my business development have helped to 'Awaken the Giant' within me at a time when it mattered most. He helped me to believe that it really was ok for me to have Giant thinking, Giant ideas and, that it was not only ok, but a necessity, if I wanted to achieve my ambitions.

Sincere thanks and appreciation also goes to Derek Arden of Derek Arden International whose continuous support and reassurance helped me to keep on keeping on.

Sincere thanks and appreciation goes to Paddy Sterrett for his business and spiritual support over the years and for giving so much of himself and time despite his own challenges.

Last, but not least, my thanks and appreciation goes to all those who provided support and feedback in the course of writing this book, especially Susan Ranger and Ifeoma Anagor for their proofing contribution and words of encouragement throughout the journey of writing this book.

Thanks to you all and anyone else who has touched my life in the business world and who have helped me to transform my thinking and abilities to be able to write this book and excel in the business world.

Jennifer

Introduction

I found writing this book helped me to consolidate my own learning and business experience as I journeyed along the path of being a new business start-up. I struggled to find my way, as I'm sure all new business start-ups do. My dream for you is that this book will help you on your journey to achieve business success. However, all this knowledge is of no use unless you use it and put it into action.

I would have loved to have had one business book that gave me a synopsis, in my language, of what I needed to know and do as a new business owner to achieve real success.

Business success is not just about business planning or market research, though they are important in their own right. The initial start-up years of a business are challenging enough without being able to discover real signposts of how to achieve your success. I guess that's why they call them 'secrets'!

More and more women are taking the plunge in starting up their own businesses and being better than men in their businesses at lasting beyond the initial two years of trial and error and the various challenges associated with this stage of business development. Women tend to work from home initially as a strategy to managing their working life and private life.

A recent research with existing businesswomen and would-be entrepreneurs (carried out by our company

Step Up! International Ltd,) reveals that getting clients and marketing their business effectively was a big challenge to 50% of women in business.

Their expectations of being in business and the reality of being in business was somewhat of a different experience. The reality of being in business brought about stress, disillusionment, unexpectedly slow growth, the need for someone to 'prod you', and more marketing challenges. 75% of all respondents said they would really value someone to talk to (for guidance) or a mentor

On the other hand, would-be businesswomen listed time; the need to maintain family life; fear and money as the main obstacles preventing them from starting their own business.

"Knowing what to do and actually putting it into action are two different things. I know if I take more action I get better results, this leads to more self belief and increased confidence –spiralling upwards all the time. Just do it!"

Barbara Oldham, Independent Distributor, Forever Living Products

As a new or young business you may not necessarily know what to do. You may not know how to do what you need to do. Don't let this stop you in your tracks. You can still be the successful entrepreneur that you want to be and deserve to be. Not knowing how to do something is not a reason or excuse for you not to do it.

Take the plunge and seek the support that you need to get it done.

Always go with what feels right for you irrespective of 'seasoned' and experienced entrepreneurs advising you what might be best for you. Get in touch with your gut instincts, your intuition and let them guide you on your journey.

In today's society I find that more and more people are searching for meaning in their lives and are exploring different avenues to find it. Women are naturally intuitive people and need to hold on to and use this gift if they want to be successful.

Successful entrepreneurs generally identify the need for long-term relationships as a crucial factor in any business becoming and staying successful. Women generally are very good at building relationships. It is these skills, together with your intuition that you need to use more in the business world, rather than lose them to compete with men.

Research by Daniel Isenberg, professor of Harvard Business School, shows that at least 80% of top managers and successful entrepreneurs use their intuition to make key decisions. In a lot of cases they do this without having any data to back up their decisions and even after having done all the planning and fact finding, their gut instincts are what ultimately prevail. Additionally, Weston Agor from the University of Texas, discovered that intuition was a skill used more often by managers higher up the managerial ladder. He concluded that intuition was a necessary skill for anyone in a leadership position.

Learning to use my intuition helped me to develop better, deeper trust in myself and, whenever I use it to make a business decision, I know I've made the right decision for me.

One piece of advice I have taken from Robert Kiyosaki, author of Rich Dad, Poor Dad, is to "learn to use your emotions to think; not think with your emotions."

Edward De Bono, guru of lateral thinking, also confirms that your feelings and intuition are important for thinking.

Born To Win is very much what I believe about myself. I firmly believe that we are sent on this earth to have particular experiences to move us on in our lives: to strengthen us. This is very much how I view all of my experiences to date – the good and not so good.

I can tell you that when I first started out in the business world that I didn't have a clue what I was doing. All I knew was that I was meant to be successful and that staying in a job was not going to bring me the success that I desired and deserved. What I can say to you is just go for it! Start where you are at and the answers that you need will come to you along the way. Being in business is about taking risks.

I know what I know now as a result of having experiences along my journey, and also because I asked for help – and got it.

The main thing is: hold onto your dreams! No matter what, do what you love to do and follow your dream, for that is where you will find peace and fulfilment. You know that you know. As Ghandi said: "Don't let anyone trample on your mind with their dirty feet." Don't let others dissuade you from your passion.

This is by no means a definitive work of what is necessary to achieve business and life success. However, use it to help you at the start or middle of your business journey. Use it if you are a business owner or entrepreneur who needs to rekindle your faith in yourself or to regain your motivation. Use it for success in your personal life.

What is right for me may not be right for you. Choose what you want from this book that works for you.

Decide for yourself how much you want your success and what price you are willing to pay to get it!

BELIEVE that you are a WINNER!

Jennifer McLeod

Chapter 1
The Power of Belief

If not you, who?
If not now, when?
If not here, where?
Anonymous

Of all the strategies designed for you to be the entrepreneur you want to be, the power of belief is by far the one strategy that will ensure you achieve your dream goals.

The more you believe in yourself the less circumstances and other people will be able to stop you in your tracks. The only limitation to you achieving anything in your life is the limitation you place on yourself. Don't allow others to feed your mind with negative thoughts. Be persistent in striving for what you want – this is an act of faith and it shows how much you believe in yourself. Every successful person has only reached their height of success by having fallen over numerous times. Remember the words of the song:

Pick yourself up, dust yourself off, and start all over again!

You have only failed if you give up.

Thomas Edison, inventor of the incandescent electric light bulb in the home succeeded in his dream after

10,000 attempts. Less than half way to achieving his dream Edison was ridiculed for persisting in his attempt to create 'electric light'. A reporter asked him why he persisted with his experiments after 5000 failed attempts when 'everyone knew' it was not possible to have electric lighting. Edison's response was 'I haven't failed. I have discovered 5000 ways of how not to do it. These can now be eliminated from my experiments.'

Winners keep on keeping on. Act through faith and courage to achieve what you want in life. When you believe that you can achieve whatever your mind and heart desires, then faith will follow.

Your riches and your success begin with a thought or an idea. Faith in yourself removes all limitations. Ask for what you want and believe that you will get it.

'Whatever the mind can conceive and believe, it can achieve'
Napoleon Hill

Universal Energy Force

There is nothing religious about this chapter. Some people may refer to that 'thing' that they believe in as the Higher Power, the Higher Self, God, Allah, or Universal Energy Force. Religion focuses on customs, rules that must be obeyed, is governed by man and places restrictions on you. Spirituality, on the other hand, is an inner knowing, oneness and alignment with the spirit or universal energy force that we are all a part of.

Spirituality enables you to be the great person you were destined to be, to be creative and to follow your purpose whilst here on earth. We are very much part of the universal life force, providing us with infinite power, if we choose to tap into it. It is available to us twenty-four hours of the day, seven days a week, three hundred and sixty five days of the year. Let go and let the universal energy flow through you. Be ready and willing to learn your lessons on the way. The power is truly within you. When you are in doubt or fear, all you need do is sit down quietly, ask the question and expect the answer you seek to come to you.

Your intuition won't tell you everything you need to know about being in business. Like everything new, you have got to take time to learn about your business, especially if it is new. However, within that, your intuition will tell you perhaps the best business route or your particular spin on a model that is true for you - a spin that is designed to give you the edge ahead of your competitors.

For instance, I had been trying to find the right niche market for my business for some time now. It was a particularly frustrating process from time to time as I had thought I had found the right niche in the past, however, this turned out not to be the case. When I eventually found my niche of working with separated or divorced women, I knew instantly that it was exactly the right one for me. It felt right and everything literally fell into place. In addition, my experience of being a divorcee myself added real value and authenticity to my work. It is a unique area of work in the UK and gives my business the edge.

It is the inner knowing and sense of peace that I now have with my business that tells me it is the right niche for me. Again, always trust your instincts.

Be, Do and Have More

We can all be, do and have so much more if we choose to.

BE

Nature's laws suggest that being successful is about being the person you want to be right now. It's not about waiting for years on end until you become that person you aspire to being. See yourself in your mind's eye being the new you.

- What do you look like?
- What colours are you wearing?
- What are you doing?
- How are you being – confident, strong, motivated, spiritual, rich?

When you are being more than you are right now, you automatically enable others around you to shine with you. There is indeed plenty in the universe for all of us. Your abundance awaits you.

Too often we allow others, or what others might say about us, to stop us being the person we know we can be and are destined to be. We mope around and blame others for what WE are not doing to make our lives better. As adults, we are all responsible for our own lives. Start taking responsibility for your life now. Take control of your life to achieve the success and happiness you want. You can if you think you can! It doesn't matter what happened yesterday, last month, last year or in your childhood. BE the person that you want to be today.

DO

Once you have identified your goal that you want to achieve, then identify the tasks or activities that you will need to undertake to become the person you want to be or the thing you want to have in your life or business.

Break the goal into smaller chunks – a bit like eating an elephant one chunk at a time. These smaller chunks become sub-goals to which you need to allocate dates. Allocating deadlines to your sub-goals as well as the overall goal will help you to achieve them. This is the process which makes achieving the goal that much easier.

This is the part of the process of goal achievement that really matters, as it is what leads to you taking action.

Action is definitely the key to getting results.

Make a plan and follow through. DO IT.

You'll find out lots more about this in chapter 4, which is all about Goal Achievement.

HAVE

When you follow through with your plan to be the new you and you take action, then you will HAVE your goals appear in your life. This is what you keep your focus on.

Too many people get the process backwards and focus on having something in their life first, then they will do it and then become it. All successful people have a very clear idea of what they will be like and what they want to have well before they have these things in place.

Tom Watson, IBM CEO knew exactly what he wanted to achieve long before it happened and went about acting as if he already had it – he acted as if IBM was already a big, successful company.

> *'If you want to improve your self image, improve your memory'*
> *Zig Ziglar*

Your self-image is what you think about yourself. The more your memory improves, the better you feel about yourself. The better you feel about yourself the more you start thinking and talking loving, positive thoughts. This has a knock-on effect on people around you.

The self-image equates to the thoughts that you programme into your subconscious mind, positive or negative. These dictate how you behave and what will manifest in your life. To erode your negative self-image requires making a decision to do so and taking positive action through affirmations, visualisations or both to re-programme your mind. Simply put, if you don't like what you are then change it. The only thing that you have total control over is your mind. No one or nothing has control over you unless you give them permission to do so.

Your subconscious mind does not know the difference between positive and negative thoughts and simply obeys whatever you feed it and goes into action to manifest it in your life. Become aware of your negative thought patterns and limiting beliefs. Affirmations can assist in overriding these patterns if repeated constantly. For affirmations to be effective, they must be short sentences or phrases in the first person, present tense and positive that you say to yourself repeatedly until it becomes a reality for you.

For instance, 'I like myself', 'I am rich'. You will get the result of whatever you programme into your mind, positive or negative, so ensure the phrase is positive in nature to get positive results.

James Allen, author of *'As a Man Thinketh'*, likens the mind to a garden – you can either take the deliberate step of planting flowers, watering and fertilising them, or you can do nothing and allow weeds to grow. On the basis that the mind can only accept one thought at a time, which one will you choose – positive or negative?

We are all powerful attraction magnets and draw things and people into our lives as a result of thoughts, ideas and wishes we have sent out into the universe. Take control of your mind today and make a conscious effort to regularly feed your mind with positive thoughts.

"We cannot control the world or what life hands us,

but we can control our reaction to it"
Viktor Frankl

Insight

I have got to where I am right now by trial and error, by falling over and picking myself up and starting over again. I certainly did not have the insight I have now at the beginning and it is only achievable by *doing* it!! Someone else telling you how it is for them does not help you have the same insight you need for your own business.

Having support from mentors as I have had and will still continue to do, however, can and does help you to overcome some of the hurdles quicker and or take a shortcut to achieving your success. You still need to take action in order for you to gain the true vision and true insight for yourself as the business world relates to you and vice versa. In a sense this is confirmation of the insight gained from you and your mentor

Soon after starting out in business I found myself in a frantic hurry to go out there and make some money. After a while I just wasn't enjoying what I was doing. Soon I lost sight of where I was going and what I was trying to do. The result was that I ended up on my first plateau.

Thankfully, I knew enough about surrendering to that spiritual power to be able to do something constructive about changing my situation. What this meant for me was that I made myself sit still for as long as it took for the answers to come to me. I thought about where I was going and what I ought to do next. The inspiration came.

Now I find myself in a state of complete surrender to that Higher Power, going with the flow and being totally happy with the inspiration for success that is coming my way.

I have no need to force my success. My inspiration is now so bountiful and, indeed, beautiful, that my challenge is to capture and act upon them all. A crucial factor in gaining this level of clarity was being able to trust and follow my intuition and feelings when certain thoughts and inspiration came through.

Start Now!

It took me about two years after I started out in business before I knew what I really wanted to do and where I really wanted to go. As Napoleon Hill, author of *Think And Grow Rich* says:

> ***'Start where you are at right now and the answers you need will come to you on your journey'.***

Boy, was he right! I always had a very strong sense of belief in my success and myself, even in times of confusion when I felt that I didn't know what I was doing. Prepare mentally for whatever you want to have happen in your life and business. In your mind, prepare yourself for all eventualities that are likely to arise. Ensure that your main focus is on achieving positive outcomes. If you fall over on your journey it is simply an inevitable bump in the road. How well you pick yourself up and learn from your mistakes is not only a testament of your character, but will also determine the actions you take thereafter to lead you to your destiny.

> *"Believe nothing because a wise man said it.*
> *Believe nothing because it is generally held*
> *Believe nothing because it is written*
> *Believe nothing because it is said to be divine*
> *Believe nothing because someone else believes it*
> *But believe only what you yourself judge to be true".*
> *Buddha*

Mental Preparation

Mental preparation is the crucial deciding factor between winners and losers. See yourself being and feeling confident in any given situation and engage in positive self-talk before any event.

See your audience applauding you at the end of a speech or envisage a handshake at the end of a deal, signalling success. The mental preparation helps the mind to reduce the obstacles and override these producing a knowing and feeling that 'YES I CAN! I'm ready and I'm a winner!'

Many athletes use this process as their winning formula. For instance, Linford Christie used this technique with the British Olympic team; and the East Germans who used to dominate sporting events years ago. This is something I do every day to keep my mind focused on my future life vision and sub-goals. For instance, my mental preparation helped me to get the house that I have now.

Mental preparation helps you to believe your achievement is very possible. It is said that Success is 70% mental preparation.

'The will to do springs from the knowledge that we can'
James Allen

My faith paid off as it was at this time when the inspiration came through for my Formula for Success. And it is this:

Jennifer McLeod's ABCD&KP Success Formula© 2006

AA - Accept and Acknowledge that you can

BB – Believe and Be Bold

CC – Conceive Your Ideas Concisely

DD – Decide and Do It

Above all else:

K - Keep your Mouth Shut

P – Play

AA - Accept and Acknowledge that you can:

In order for you to move ahead in your life and achieve the success you desire and deserve, you must first accept and acknowledge that you ARE capable of achieving it. The very fact that the universe provided you with the thought or inspiration is a sign of its faith in your ability to achieve it. This is your foundation level. It is your platform from which you will be transformed.

BB – Believe and Be Bold:

This is the stage where, no matter what else is happening in your life or business, you need to have undying and unfailing faith and belief in yourself. You are what you think you are. Be Bold about trying out new ideas to move you closer to achieving your success. If something doesn't work, then try something else – take your learning from it and move on.

CC – Conceive Your Ideas Concisely:

Be clear about what you want. Woolly ideas produce woolly results so be clear and accurate about what you are aiming for. Then break down your BIG Goals into small manageable chunks. Chunk it!

DD – Decide And Do It:

Whilst decision-making appears at this stage in my Success Formula, it is by no means a subsidiary process. Decide what you want. Decide that you will do it and go for it! DO IT. And then keep going.

K – Keep Your Mouth Shut

Yes, this is blunt. Why? I think *sometimes the message needs to be blunt or repeated several times and in different ways for people to hear it.* Keeping your goals confidential is a sure way of ensuring that you get there. Talking too much about what you want to do to too many people, will either tell the person you are talking to how much or how little you really do know. It puts them in a position to capture your ideas and put them into effect before you even get started yourself.

Keeping your goals confidential means you won't be giving negative people opportunities to dampen your spirits on your journey by telling you that you can't achieve your goals. Only share your goals with people who are likely to say 'Yes! Go For It!' and 'Great! How can I help you?'

P – Play

This stage in my Success Formula can mean anything you attach to the word play. It could be taking time out with your family, leisure or hobby activities, working on your lifetime goals. Basically, it's anything that allows you to take time away from work. It is anything that makes your heart sing; that brings you to life. For me, this is singing, painting or dancing.

Playing is a crucial stage in enabling you to achieve success. It assists in stress reduction, it helps you to develop a better relationship with yourself and others and it stimulates your subconscious mind, sometimes referred to as your super-conscious mind.

"Your behaviour is based upon your feelings, which are based on your thoughts. So the thing to work on is not to change your behaviour, but those things inside of your consciousness that we call thoughts. Once your thoughts reflect what you genuinely want to be, the appropriate

emotions and the consequent behaviour will flow automatically. Believe it, and you will see it".
Dr Wayne Dyer

Self-Belief

Constant never-ending belief in yourself is what is required. When 'they' are telling you that you 'can't', you need to be there for you, affirming '**Yes, I Can**'. It is very easy to lose one's way or become disempowered and disillusioned if you don't have that unfailing belief in yourself.

"Whether you think you can, or whether you think you can't – either way you're right,"
Henry Ford'

Be a 'Henry Ford' who insisted on having the kind of car he wanted irrespective of the length of time it would take for his workforce to find the answers to make it happen. All winners find a way. There must be a way for you to succeed. Find it, and most importantly believe that you can. Do not allow other people's opinions to sway you and divert you from where you need to be.

"You see things as they are and say why? But I dream things that never were and say why not?"
George Bernard Shaw

The more I continued in faith, the more the answers came to me and people were being sent to me to help me on my journey. I know that the people around me supporting me in my business now are not here by accident.

Let me tell you about something that happened to me.

I had been sent a brochure for a big conference in the post that I hadn't been able to go to. The following year's event was a big event celebrating the 10th Anniversary of that particular conference and I really wanted to be able to speak then. I picked up the phone to try and find out how I could do this. To my surprise I was put through to the Managing Director.

"Good morning," he said, "what can I do for you?"

"I've been reading about your conference and I'd really like to speak next year. What do I need to do to take part?" I asked.

"Just send us a synopsis of your speech and how you intend to involve the audience. Send it as soon as you can before the bulk of the applications arrive in the autumn," he replied.

Well, I did just that!

On that same day, I intended to identify one of the speakers in the brochure who had spoken the previous year. I wondered about the possibility of a strategic alliance with that person.

Before I had chosen one of the previous speakers to contact, I checked my emails. I couldn't believe it! I had an email from one of the previous speakers at the conference regarding a product from my website. I felt sure that this was divine intervention. I emailed her back.

"Funny you should send me an email today. I was just looking at last year's brochure to see who I wanted to contact about a possible alliance. I hadn't made a decision yet," I said.

"Well, it was purely by accident that I came across your website. In any case, I too am a believer in life's greater plan," she said

We made arrangements to contact each other again.

I did not get a response for a good while after sending off the application form for the conference speaking engagement. However, one day, out of the blue I received an email and a phone call to say that I was one of the chosen speakers who would be speaking with some of the founding speakers of the conference.

You can imagine how excited I was. I felt sure that I was meant to be there.

My all knowing, internal tutor always knows what is best for me.

Failure to use the information and consistently ignoring the wisdom given by your inner spirit, teaches it not to give you too much inspiration because it is aware of them not being acted upon. The wisdom and the frequency of inspiration diminish, but doesn't go away totally. When you are ready to act, they will make themselves available to you.

> ***"It is emotional intelligence that motivates us to pursue our unique potential and purpose, and activates our***

innermost values and aspirations, transforming them from things we think about to what we live".
Robber K. Cooper and Ayman Sawaf

Examples of successful people who kept their faith in themselves no matter what include:

- The founder of Kentucky Fried Chicken (KFC), Colonel Harland Sanders, who was rejected nearly a thousand times for his idea.

- Sylvester Stallone star of Rocky films who was told by every film producer and director he approached that he would never make it as an actor. He had a paradigm shift and produced and co-starred in his own film with his dog.

- Arthur Ashe, the only top Black tennis player in his day, focused solely on his outcome rather than people's reaction to his colour.

- Oprah Winfrey is today the richest person in the entertainment industry, despite being a Black woman growing up in her time and despite her childhood experiences.

- Henry Ford had his vision of his T model car that had to be built with particular specifications and took his workforce a whole year to find the answers as to how to build it. Henry Ford remained resolute in his decision that that was what he wanted and that the solution was out there somewhere. For a whole year, he ignored the media and his workforce telling him it could not be done. The rest is history.

Always go along with what is right for you. Sometimes it may be just a feeling that is difficult to explain to others, and even if you were able to explain it, others may still find your explanation difficult to comprehend. Stick with it!

> *Honour your own values system, because the deeply personal elements make the work satisfying. When it doesn't feel right, there's a reason for it."*
> *Bill Malloy, Former CEO of Peapod*

First Thoughts

First thing on waking up, I make every effort to capture my first thoughts. Sometimes I make a note of them in my daily journal to help me to remember them after I engage in the hustle and bustle of the day. In the event that I don't write them down, I make every attempt to follow through with the first thought that I awoke with that day and take action to implement it.

The first thought might be the solution to a situation you had been looking for or it may be the solution to a challenge that you hadn't realised consciously that you had. The subconscious mind, however, is constantly working throughout your sleep to find and give you the answers to your predominant thoughts. This could be in the form of dreams, ideas, or inspirations.

I don't question this first thought anymore and go to work on the idea throughout the day as a priority task knowing that it is the best thing for me to concentrate my efforts on that day. Generally I have learnt to follow and trust my first thoughts as they are there to guide, protect and support me. They are your truth and the tendency is for people to rationalise these ideas to make them 'fit' their mindset and their experience.

Additionally, for the first hour of each and every day I take the opportunity to connect with my inner spirit and the universal energy force. I meditate and sometimes as I am doing so, **I experience the sensation of my whole body and mind literally coming together in alignment.** This is particularly the case if I wake up earlier than normal or if I go to bed very late. I then continue with what Tony Robbins refers to as 'Hour of Power'.

This can be anything that helps you connect with yourself more. For me this includes prayer, healing, reading and writing out my goals, reading affirmations and exercise. I have a pen and notepad by my bed to capture ideas and inspirations last thing at night or first thing in the morning. Having a notepad available to you last thing at night is particularly useful to off-load ideas you have going round in your head just before you go off to sleep. It is a fantastic remedy for insomnia.

Imaginary Committee

Another method I use to find solutions to difficult situations is to have an imaginary committee as unveiled by Napoleon Hill in his book *'Think and Grow Rich'*. It is another excellent way of developing trust in your intuition and ultimately in yourself. I have found solutions to any challenge come to me straightaway when I pose the question to my role models as to how best to deal with the situation. It is also an excellent way of getting support from high profile people and role models that you may not otherwise have access to.

I use the process whenever there is a need, however some people use it last thing at night just before going to sleep, enabling the subconscious to bring about the answers they need in the morning. Be open-minded about having unexpected high profile people popping up on your committee offering their wisdom to you.

The process is as follows:

Take a few deep breaths

Identify the role models you want to have on your imaginary committee and the qualities they have that you find particularly appealing. See them in your mind's eye.

When a situation arises that you find a challenge, sit quietly and ask each of your role models in turn and by name, what advice they have for dealing with that situation. For instance, two of my role models are Oprah Winfrey and Richard Branson. If I have a situation to deal with, I would visualise Oprah or Richard and ask, "Oprah, how would you deal with this?" or "Richard, how could I solve this?"

Expect to get an answer. If the answer doesn't come straightaway, continue on your journey with the expectation that the answers will be given to you.

Be open-minded about the solutions that are given. They will generally be the best solutions for you. Trust.

If you are unsure of how to implement the solutions, ask your committee. That's what they are there for.

Write down the solutions given.

"Within you right now is the power to do things you never dreamed possible. This power becomes available to you just as soon as you can change your beliefs."
Dr Maxwell Maltz

Abundance Mentality

Developing an abundance mentality is absolutely vital in moving forward and realising your dreams. You must change in order for higher-level goodness to come to you. If you don't change, there will be a mismatch and it is unlikely that abundance will come to you. If it does happen, you will not be able to sustain it until you change your thinking, as your mindset would still be at a lower level of acceptance.

So, for instance, you may have a very good income, but have nothing to show for it and never seem to have any money. This could be because, at a subconscious level, you are telling yourself that you don't deserve to have financial abundance or that you are not good enough.

Law of Attraction

The Law of Attraction suggests that we attract people and circumstances into our lives as a direct result of what's going on at a subconscious level in your mind. In order to attract different people and different circumstances into your life, you will need to feed your mind with new positive images and new information.

This is sometimes referred to as Karma, or 'what goes around, comes around'.

Nature only gives us what we need when we are ready. Get Ready! Do not allow obstacles to stop you in your tracks in seeking your true purpose in life. The experience of 'not knowing' can sometimes be frustrating and confusing, however, it is not an excuse to stop or not start at all. Deciding to do something does not require you to know how to achieve it at the beginning of your journey.

> ***"Before a person can accomplish anything of an enduring nature in the world she must first of all acquire some measure of success in the management of your own mind. If a person cannot govern the forces within herself, she cannot hold a firm hand upon the outer activities that form her visible life".***
> ***The Mastery Destiny***

As soon as you get an idea or inspiration, act on it. If you don't, you will lose it. How often have you had an idea and thought to yourself 'I must write that down', and an hour or so later you are desperately trying to remember it. I promise you that if you let go and follow your intuition, your life and your business will be so much better and easier. **Following your intuition will save you time and money and a whole lot of energy.**

Using Your Intuition

There are numerous benefits to be gained from using your intuition. These include:

- Becoming stress free
- Acquiring peace in your life
- Finding your true, authentic self
- Losing your inhibitions
- Giving yourself permission to accept and embrace the abundance that awaits you.

"You have within you an inner guidance that always knows what you need to do. Trusting this inner guidance will set you free and help you to move the obstacles that you once considered to be mountains."
Jennifer McLeod

Using your intuition will foster greater creativity within you, enabling you to use your right brain more effectively, releasing a flow of energy that will bring about a fusion of mind, body and spirit alignment to move you closer to achieving your success.

Great leaders like Thomas Edison, always follow their intuition. As pointed out earlier, it took 10,000 attempts before Thomas Edison had his final breakthrough. Yet how did he know that this was possible? It was a combination of desire, belief and intuition that kept him going.

In-Tuition

Intuition is simply what it says: ***In-tuition.*** It is an inner guidance and inner tutor that guides your thoughts and actions if you let it. You have the same intuitive, genius abilities as our great leaders. They are more latent in some of us than in others.

Intuition is not logic. It provides you with no rhyme or reason as to why you should do what you are doing. It is connected to your heart and emotions and just is. It is there to guide you to do and say what is best for you and to help you to become your true, authentic self - the **REAL YOU**.

It is generally when you do not follow your intuition that something in your business or in your life will go wrong. It is there to protect you. Your intuition may manifest itself in different ways. For instance, you might get a particular feeling about something, see images or hear things

Check Your Intuition

Allow your intuition or body to guide you in finding the answers to the following questions. Don't use your head or logic. Sit quietly in solitude and ask yourself the following:

- In relation to my business, **am I doing what I love to do**? Feel where the answer is in your body. Getting an uncomfortable feeling at this stage is a general indication that you are not doing what you love to do

- What is it that I love to do?

Feel it! With your mind's eye, imagine yourself doing it. Visualise yourself achieving your goal. Then make a plan towards achieving it

Think of a business project that you are working on right now or will be embarking on or the future direction of your business.

- How does the future of the business feel?

- Is it going in the right direction? **Feel the answer.** What images do you see?

If your intuition suggests your business is not going in the right direction, ask it what you need to do to move it in the right direction.

Use all of your senses to direct you to the best way forward.

"Intuition is the new physics. It's an Einsteinian, seven-sense, practical way to make tough decisions. The crazier the times are, the more important it is for leaders to develop and trust their intuition."
Tom Peters

Emotion

You need to get emotional with your intuition. Allow yourself to feel your emotion. Intuition is an emotional force. We are all naturally intuitive beings. Your intuition is you and it is the part of you that Western society ignores at the expense of placing more of an emphasis on logic and what can be scientifically proven. Intuition is neither logic nor intelligence.

Developing intuition is a process that will take time, faith and practice and a lot of trust from you, especially if it is something that you are not used to. It is not based on others telling you what to do. It is an experience that only you can have for yourself, which will be a different experience and feeling from anyone else's experience of their intuitive self. What feels, looks and sounds right for you may not be right for anyone else. It is a process that embraces all of your senses, if you allow it to do so.

Give yourself permission to have this truly, beautiful, serene, rich, peaceful experience that is rightfully yours. It will make all the difference to your life and your business.

Mahatma Ghandi meditated from Sunday midnight right through to Monday midnight in total solitude, without drink or food. It is the inspirations he gained from this process that enabled him to defeat the British army in a totally non-violent manner. Mother Teresa's greatness was magnified by the fact that she allowed her intuition to take her to where she was needed. She was revered by Heads of States across the globe for what she 'felt' she needed to do.

Let Your Intuition Be Your Best Friend

I now trust my intuition implicitly and know that, whatever messages it sends me in whatever form, it is generally the best thing for me to do. It is my best friend. Let your intuition become your best friend.

I have used it to back out of some deals and what, on the face of it, seemed to be some good business ventures. Sometimes I am unable to explain why I am not able to go forward with a particular activity, however, these days it does not concern me that I don't know. I am just satisfied and grateful that I have been forewarned about the situation not being in my best interest before it occurred. It is on those occasions when I ignored my intuition that I got myself into hot water.

Now, if it does happen, instead of wishing I had follow my intuition, I simply analyse what happened and whether I was in fact aware of the warning signs before the situation arose. For example, recently I pulled out of a contract with a business coach.

There were two alarm bells (and possibly more) that I had overlooked. The alarm bells were camouflaged by the fact that I had met this business coach in a very giving, positive, happy, supportive environment of high calibre business people.

It was during a networking break at an annual conference that I started talking to one of the conference delegates who was a business coach. We decided to meet up after the conference for business coaching sessions.

"Just phone the office and I'll ask one of the girls to book you an appointment", he said. At the time when he said this a little flutter occurred in my stomach (first warning sign ignored).

Another delegate walked with us and it was evident from her facial expressions that she too had picked upon what he had said.

I agreed to meet up with him. He invited me to one of his free preview business sessions which was very good. I heard another alarm bell when he spoke to 'one of the girls' in his team at the event (second warning sign ignored). The positive energy from the conference was still flowing between us, thus serving to camouflage the real situation.

After a separate introductory session which I thought went well, I agreed to work with him. The next session and first of the contract, left me totally drained of energy and demoralised, so much so that it took me several days to shake off the effects. There was a lot of negative projection onto me which also included him telling me that I couldn't achieve certain goals or sub goals.

I ended the contract and requested my money back as he offered a money back guarantee on his services. He declined my request as he thought his coaching had worked. Some communication followed which was not too pleasant.

Whilst I lost some money in the process, it was definitely cheaper to have lost it at that stage than further down the road.

After the experience I analysed if I had been made aware of potential alarm bells previous to the contract taking place. After some thought I realised the answer was 'Yes'.

As you learn to trust your intuition, and essentially yourself, I promise you that your confidence level will increase. All successful people have got to where they are now by using their intuition, their instincts, gut feeling or inner spiritual guidance.

Intuition Exercise:

Ask yourself:

- When do I recognise my intuition?
- What am I generally doing when it happens?
- How does my intuition manifest itself?
- Am I aware that I am overriding or ignoring my intuition? What do I do when this happens?
- How does my body talk to me intuitively?
    - Do I get ringing sound in my ears?
    - Do I get physical sensations in my stomach? Gut feelings?
    - Does a feeling of calmness come over me when I know it is the right thing for me to do?
    - Do I have an instant dislike to someone I've only just met?

You can increase your intuition or super-conscious ability by:

- Listening to any baroque or classical music, e.g. Mozart or Beethoven
- Doing relaxation exercises
- Going into silence and solitude
- Undertaking a workshop with yourself – where you write a question on paper and allow your mind to free flow to find the answers and solutions you require.

- Following your first thoughts every time.

How You Can Use This Six Step Model to Achieve Success

1. Make the decision today to start trusting yourself and your intuition

2. Take time to recognise your predominant form of receiving intuition

3. Follow through no matter what. This is the only way for you to begin to learn and to take baby steps towards greater trust in yourself

4. Visualise your goals daily

5. Meditate regularly

6. Find stillness every day to connect with you, your inner spirit.

Chapter 2
How To Develop A Better Relationship With Yourself

"If you work hard on your business, you will make lots of money. If you work hard on you, you will make a fortune."
Jim Rohn

The chapter on Power of Belief, especially, and other parts of this book, go a long way to assist you in developing a better relationship with yourself. This chapter will take you even further by providing more tools and techniques.

People buy people first – not your product, business or services. People must be able to like and trust *you first* before they are able to do business with you. Jordan Productions, US research shows that up to 83% of sales are lost if you do not have a good relationship with your customers.

In order for you to have a good relationship with your customers, you must first have a good relationship with yourself. In order to develop successful relationships you need to like yourself.

Whilst it is not to necessary to like everyone as an entrepreneur or business owner, it is essential that you learn to like your customers, as successful businesses are built on having long-term relationship with your customers or relational clients.

It is far easier to sell to an existing customer than to a new one. To ensure that you are someone that customers come back to, it is imperative for you to either already have a good relationship with yourself or be actively engaged in developing a better one. Jordan Productions, US research shows that all successful entrepreneurs spend an absolute minimum of £12,000 per annum on their own personal development.

David Sandler, top sales guru, says that YOU are by far the most important aspect of your business; more important than the market and more important than the business itself.

Attitude + Behaviour + Technique will ensure your success, providing that you continue on a journey of continuous self-improvement.

The attitude is how you see yourself, your self-image and your general outlook on life. It starts from the moment you wake up: what are the first thoughts that enter your mind?

"Oh, today is going to be a tough day,"

"I wish I didn't have to work today"?

These can be changed if you become aware of them and say to yourself that

"Today is the best day yet".

You know what you say to yourself, so have some positive self-talk ready to power up your day.

The techniques are the skills that you will require to run the business to bring about your success. The importance of how you feel inside about yourself cannot be stressed enough, and therefore the inclusion of this chapter on developing a better relationship with yourself.

To help customers and others to develop trust in you:

- Be congruent in all that you do and say. Your customers will spot any inconsistencies sooner rather than later.

- Keep your word and do all you say you will do.

- Say what you mean and mean what you say.

Remember people buy you first before looking at your product or services. One of the key things that I have learnt in business in this respect is to under-promise and over-deliver.

Let's look at some of the tools that you can use to develop a better relationship with yourself.

Permission

Give yourself permission to be successful. Most often than not, it will be you stopping yourself from achieving the success you deserve, by allowing negative beliefs to prevail. There really is abundance in the universe for everyone, you included.

Successful people take control of their lives and create their own successes. They don't just sit back and let things happen to them. What success means to you may not be success for others; everyone has their own idea of what success means for them. So what does success mean for you?

> *"One would assume that if you are loved by so many, you would love yourself. But this is not always true. It's not true for most of us … love has to come from within, if it is to come at all".*
> *Elizabeth Kubler-Ross, Life Lessons*

Get rid of the old habit, situation or stories you tell yourself that are stopping you from achieving your success. For instance,

"I'm not good enough",

"Nothing good ever happens to me",

"I'll never be successful",

"I'll never be rich."

These are all called limiting beliefs and they focus your mind on lack. It is only when you start talking positively to yourself (interrupting the pattern and old habits) that your focus will shift, helping you to find new ways of having positive, successful experiences. It is this new positive paradigm shift that will enable you to move forward. If this last stage does not occur, the likelihood is that the old habit will reappear before long.

So what do you do?

You start all over again and resolve to make it stick next time.

> *"Get yourself out of the way so the REAL YOU can get going!"*
> *Jennifer McLeod*

Own up to your 'stuff'. Acknowledge it and get rid of it. When you are able to let yourself go, then you will be able to empower and let others go too. In order to be successful in your business ventures you must be willing to look at how you are limiting yourself and be absolutely honest with yourself about the areas you need to improve in and on.

This is a most crucial step. If you don't identify the areas of your performance that need attention, it will definitely hold you back. Seek assistance from someone, a Coach or Mentor, who is willing to assist you in identifying these areas. Then do something about it.

> *"Empowerment is all about letting go so that others can get going."*
> *Kenneth Blanchard, The One Minute Manager*

Stop being 'nice' just to please other people – just be yourself! Find your unique self and flaunt it!

- Who are you?
- What are you about?
- What is special about you?
- What do you do best?
- How do you do it?

That's what sells YOU. When you are honest with yourself, then and only then can you be honest with your customers and clients.

Entrepreneurs like Richard Branson are able to be in a position of 'Ready, Fire, Aim' only if they have a good relationship with themselves. This means that this type of entrepreneur has already 'fired' whilst others are still 'aiming'. They then review to see if they have hit the target, reposition themselves if they haven't and fire again. That is why this type of entrepreneur is always ahead of the game because they are not only prepared to take the risk time and time again, but have the confidence within themselves to sort it if it goes wrong.

Richard Branson's self-belief, trust and confidence in himself led him, and ultimately Virgin airlines, to win the airline dispute with British Airways. British Airways at the time was a much bigger and established competitor in the airline business.

You must trust that what you are doing is the right thing for you to do, irrespective of the outcome. You must have *faith in you.*

Self Worth

As Peter Thomson of PTI International once said to me, **"you're charging the price for your life."** That is to say, it is your life experiences that you are charging people for. At the time, my initial response was "I don't want to overcharge people". He then explained that no one else has had the experiences that I have had, nor sees things the way I do as a result of having had these experiences. Consequently you charge for your services accordingly.

Tony Robbins charges in the region of $100,000 per day.

When I first started out as a self-employed businesswoman, I was simultaneously holding down a part-time job, a degree course, a single parent; and still able to fit in some short personal and professional development courses each lasting several months. These, together with all my life experiences – good and bad – have taken me to where I am now.

Looking back at my past and the knowledge that I've acquired as a result of my experiences, it wasn't long before I made the necessary paradigm shift to charge for my services accordingly.

So, you are charging according to the value you place on yourself, your experiences, knowledge and skills.

Your focus should always be on how you can develop yourself to enable you to deliver better services or products to your clients. That is, a better service that will add more value and greater benefits to meet the clients needs. How can you help your clients to be more successful?

What you are worth is a decision *you* need to make not the market. Then you go to work to show your customers why you are worth what you say you are worth. This is when you not only tell your customers what extra value and benefits you can add to their businesses, but also ensure that you deliver. The key to success is to deliver more than you say you will – go the extra mile.

Your Environment Is A Reflection Of You

It was only when I started interacting with entrepreneurs as opposed to getting advice from Business Advisors that things changed for me. I talked to people who were achievers and began to live the philosophies of achievers and things started to fall into place. It is immersion in this environment that helped me to adopt the necessary mindset for success. It may feel uncomfortable, at first, being in the environment of people who are more advanced in their business success than yourself, however, this is where you need to be in order to acquire the learning you need to be successful. As they say, 'birds of a feather flock together'. It may even mean paying to get into this environment, but that's business and an investment in your future success!

> *"If you don't like what you are change it"*
> *Zig Ziglar*

To find out if you are in the right environment or not, think of your ten closest associates. Divide their income by ten and this will give you an indication of your own wealth. If you want to be successful, you need to frequent places, such as seminars, that successful people frequent. Find someone who has done what you want to do and model on their success.

If you want to be a millionaire, act like a millionaire. Before long you will start to take on the characteristics of a millionaire and will be perceived and treated as such. As a consequence, you will have entered the millionaire environment and perhaps open to opportunities that may have been beyond your wildest of dreams.

Push through your fear and get into positive environments that are currently outside of your comfort zone. Sticking with the uneasiness of being with this crowd will soon dissipate and soon you will be one of them.

Being in the right environment cannot be stressed enough. As you move out and up to another level, others around you may try to hold you back to maintain the status quo. People may feel threatened by your progress or success, however, that is their issue and not yours. Move on anyway. If you want to fly, you will need to lose excess baggage.

Your personal and business environment is a direct reflection of what is going on inside your head. If you don't like what you see, change it. As the title of a well-known book goes: 'Mind Your Own Business.' This is one of the key phrases that Robert Kiyosaki, author of *Rich Dad, Poor Dad* constantly repeats. That is, stay focused on you, your business and on what you are doing.

> *"Your staying small does not serve the world".*
> *Marianne Williamson*

As I journeyed on my development, I was thankful that I had met inspiring and supportive people who knew about the power of sharing and giving freely.

Napoleon Hill in his classic *Think and Grow Rich* suggests to get a Mastermind Group of people around you as you develop to help you achieve your definite plan. Additionally, you need to consider what you will give back to this group for services rendered to you. You and your Mastermind Group must be in harmony with each other for it to be successful. Remember it is *your* Mastermind Group to support *you*. Allow the group to stretch you.

I currently have two growth buddies and three different mentors. This allows me time to be selective in formulating my Mastermind Group with people with whom I'm in harmony and that I can trust to do what is necessary to push me forward.

To put any relationship to the test, personal or professional, ask yourself,

"Is this relationship worthy of me?"

Asking this question rather than "am I worthy of any of the relationships?" puts you in a position of power. You can choose to stay with the current relationship or go. This question can be used in relation to anything, for instance, your business, goals, actions, your personal life.

> *"To attract attractive people, you must be attractive. To attract powerful people, you must be powerful. To attract committed people, you must be committed. Instead of going to work on them, you go to work on yourself. If you become, you can attract".*
> *Jim Rohn*

Choose your friends wisely, including friends that you can learn from. Whilst you are not able to choose your family, you can certainly choose how you interact with them and how you allow them to interact with you to a certain extent.

We make arrangements with ourselves and other people that we do not keep and surround ourselves with people and situations that totally devalue and limit us. It is no surprise, therefore, that we begin to lose confidence and stay in that state.

No matter who you are or what other people think of you, you must first work on yourself to eradicate the limiting beliefs you place on yourself. You are what you see. You are what you say. Become aware of these now and allow the REAL YOU to shine.

Mind Your Language

"If I were to say the things that I say to myself to my friends, I wouldn't have any friends left."
Princess Diana

James Allen in his book *As a Man Thinketh* highlights the importance of positive powerful thoughts. Whatever you say to yourself, whether silently or aloud, will depict the experience you will have. What limiting things do you say to yourself on a daily basis? What excuses are you prepared to accept, that helps you to stay stuck?

For instance, are you always saying things like:

'I can't have this because. .'?

'I can't do this because. .'?

'They won't let me. .'?

'I haven't got the brains to do that!'?

'I'm not old enough. .'?

Constantly affirm the positives. Talk about the positives; focus on your end goal. Become aware of how much time you give up to gossiping per day or week. What you give out comes back to you – guaranteed. There is no time frame for this to happen in terms of days, months or years, however, it will happen.

Automobile University

This is an expression from the US that I really like. Essentially, most people have cars these days and spend varying degrees of time travelling. What better way to use that valuable time than to spend it learning something new, or revisiting something you already covered, in an audio programme.

Successful people see themselves as self-improvement projects and are always looking for ways to improve their performance or self-image. New habits take approximately 21 – 30 days to form. Leveraging time spent travelling by car or by other means can help you to achieve this goal.

Get Organised

Being organised at home and at work is a fundamental step in moving ahead to achieving your success. In this context, being organised means developing your systems.

At home, it means organising the whole family and developing systems for everyone. This encourages individual family members to take responsibility for every aspect of chores associated with having and managing a home. For instance, within my household we all have responsibility for certain chores and tasks. Because we have all chosen them ourselves, including the children – two boys aged 15 and 10 – we all have more commitment to follow through with them. If one of the children decides they no longer wish to continue to do their chosen task, the other always reminds him that 'You chose it!' This usually has the effect of stopping the conversation very abruptly in its tracks. That aside, we re-organise on average three times per year.

I find this organisation in the home absolutely invaluable in assisting me to focus on my business. It will do the same for you too. Stephen Covey covers this in more detail in *The 7 Habits of Highly Effective People*.

In relation to being organised in your business, set up systems and test them yourself. Testing them tells you how well they work. Record all the information and then share the information with all members of your team.

By systems, I mean policies, procedures and guidelines for your company, highlighting how you do what you do in each area. So, for instance, systems for telephone calls, finance, sales, marketing, administration, training and development for your team, including team meetings.

Listen To Your Body

Your body speaks to you every day. Pay attention to what it is saying and take the appropriate action. This will not only ensure that you remain healthy, but will also assist you in being the best you can be.

I am generally a morning person, however over the years, whilst working part-time as an employee, part-time in the business and studying, I had become someone who could function at night in order to get things done.

I completed my degree alongside three or four short courses, lasting anything up to a year, whilst being a single parent as well. Somehow I managed to fit them all in as I was very clear where I wanted to get to (though not always clear about how to do it). This meant going to bed in the early hours of the morning and getting up in the early hours of the morning.

Now my body is telling me that I need to revert back to what suits it best: bed about half past eleven or midnight the latest which means that I can feel totally refreshed to awaken the early hours of the following morning. Just that half an hour difference makes all the difference to my body getting sufficient sleep and me feeling refreshed in the morning.

As I woman, I would say to all the women business owners who are reading this book, do what works for you and don't try to compete with others to make it happen. We all have different circumstances, and, whilst I would not use any of my particular circumstances to prevent me from achieving my success, it is still necessary to bear it in mind and take it into consideration when making decisions. This might simply be a case of ensuring that childcare arrangements are available, for instance. Get your support systems in place.

Life Purpose

Identify your life purpose by going with the flow of what you love to do. Ask yourself high quality, powerful questions on an ongoing basis until you get an answer of what your life purpose is supposed to be.

I firmly believe that we are all here on earth for a particular purpose. What is it that you love to do? You could also get this answer by regular meditation, asking the questions and waiting for the answers to come. Expect to get an answer, as it will come, providing you are open and receptive to it.

If you are still not sure what this is, it is likely to be that thing that, when you think about it, gives you a fantastic sensation in your body, a sparkle that makes you come alive. That's likely to be your life purpose. Until you do what you are meant to be doing whilst here on earth or even something that you love to do, you are not being true to yourself nor are you living your life to the full as nature intended.

As you continue to do what you love to do, this undoubtedly will not only inspire you and others, but will also provide us with satisfaction, peace and fulfilment. My life purpose is to teach and educate. It is what I love to do and love to see nothing better than the difference I make to other people's lives as they develop and grow as a result of my intervention.

Life Vision

Your life vision, on the other hand, is something that you want to achieve or have in your life over a period of time. This is where your focus needs to be in terms of helping you to achieve successes in your life. What vision will you use to keep you motivated when the going gets tough?

If you haven't already done so, begin to think about what your (-) dash will represent for you when you leave this planet. What will the (-) dash between your date of birth and date of death on your gravestone mean for you whilst you were on this earth? That is, what will you have achieved throughout your life that you will want to be proud of?

- What legacy do you want to leave behind?
- What do you want people to say about you at your funeral?

- When will you have accomplished what you set out to accomplish?

My life vision is in separate phases. My plan is to achieve Phase One of my vision by the year 2013, when Phase Two begins. This keeps me focused on my future and every action I take is with the intention of achieving my life vision.

Michael Gerber covers this excellently in his book *The E Myth Revisited*. He refers to life vision as your primary aim in your life.

Constantly work on your own happiness and success. It is your responsibility to do this and not anyone else's. When you do you will begin to find more meaning in your life and the whole reason and purpose of your being in business will become even clearer. Go with the flow. This is similar to what psychologist Csikszentmihayl refers to as 'flow' experience.

Be in touch with that part of yourself that is in alignment with the infinite power. Various methods such as meditation, relaxation, yoga, massages, visualisation, reading and vacations all assist in helping you to ground yourself as well as getting in touch with your sense of self.

Booking time in your diary for yourself ('me time') to be with yourself is absolutely crucial and is a way of acknowledging that you are the most important person in your world. It's about honouring yourself.

As Nigel Risner, International Speaker, suggests, if you want to live a happy life, then you MUST spend some time deciding what you want to do with your life, and then make the effort to live that life with passion.

Consider the following powerful and high quality questions compiled by Nigel Risner, to help you identify your life vision or your life purpose:

1. What is my life's purpose?
2. If I had to take a best guess at my life's purpose, what would it be?
3. Who am I?
4. What is the most important thing in my life?
5. What do I love to do, more than anything else?
6. If I had only six months left to live, what would I like to achieve?
7. What would I like to leave the world, as my legacy?
8. What would I do with my life, if I knew I could not fail?
9. If money, or time, or current responsibilities were not an issue, what would I like to do with my life, more than anything else in the world?
10. What activities have I discovered that give me the most pleasure?
11. What do I still want to learn?
12. When I was a child, what did I dream of doing with my life?

13. What has been the greatest challenge that I have overcome so far in my life? Could I help other people to overcome that same challenge?

14. What challenge would I love to overcome, and then help others achieve the same?

15. Who are the people I most admire?

16. Why do I admire these people?

17. How would I define their life's purpose?

18. What qualities do these people possess that I'd also like to be known for?

19. What is the biggest dream I have ever had for my life?

20. What subjects did I enjoy most in school?

21. What sport have I most enjoyed?

22. What art or craft have I most enjoyed?

23. What social activity have I most enjoyed?

24. What hobbies have I pursued?

25. What hobbies do I wish I had pursued?

26. What would I like to do, if only other people didn't think it was silly?

27. Where in the world would I most like to live?

28. Who would I like to live there with?

29. Where in the world would I like to work?

30. Who would I most like to work with?

31. What would my perfect day be like?

32. Is there a spiritual side to me, waiting to be unleashed?

33. What would I like to do, RIGHT NOW, which would bring me the most happiness or pleasure?

34. What special gift do I have that I could give to the world?

35. What makes me cry with joy, or brings tears to my eyes?

36. What would I like to do this weekend, just for fun?

37. If I could be granted the power to change the world, what would I do?

38. If I were given three wishes, what would they be?

39. What is something that scares me a bit, but would be really exciting if I did it?

40. What does my heart say I am to do with my life?

41. What qualities do I possess that I am really proud of?

42. What have I done in my life that I am really proud of?

43. If I had time available to contribute to a charity, or some cause, what would it be?

44. What am I usually doing when I suddenly realise that time has flown by, and all my focus has been on that one task?

45. What do I want to do on my next vacation?

46. Who in history would I most love to be, and why?

47. What do I most regret not doing, so far in my life?

48. At the end of my life, what would I most regret not having done?

49. What is my life's purpose?

50. If I had to take a best guess at my life's purpose, and just get started with something that excites me, what would it be?

How You Can Use This Chapter To Achieve Your Success

- As of today give yourself permission to succeed. You deserve it.

- Think about your life experiences and the journey you have travelled to get you to where you are now. Use it to help you to value your worth.

- Get uncomfortable today. Get into different environments that are likely to stretch you and bring you into contact with like-minded people.

- Get organised at home and in your business. Identify a plan of action and follow it.

- Become aware of the negative stories you constantly tell yourself that are holding you back. Replace these stories with positive self-talk.

- Identify your life vision. What do you want to accomplish?

- What is your purpose on this earth? What is it that you were sent here to do?

Chapter 3
How To Get Rid Of Fear And Get On With Your Business And Your Life

"It is in your moments of decision that your destiny is shaped."
Anthony Robbins

What is fear? FEAR is often said to stand for False Evidence Appearing Real. Check it out. How real is the situation that you fear so much?

Too often we allow fear to stand in the way of our success and we rationalise our ideas away. That same idea that could be your winning idea!

Ask For Help

I am naturally a cautious person and have had to learn to let go of a lot of my caution in order to move ahead in the business world. The caution is embedded in fear. I have pushed myself to overcome the fear of rejection so I can ask for help. The more I asked, the more I got it. Now I feel totally comfortable asking literally anyone in the business world for help.

My experience is that many new and young businesses do not ask for help often enough nor do they ask the right people. Asking the right people for help was absolutely the key turning point for me. The right people are people who you feel you can work with; who are willing to share their experiences; and who, but not necessarily, have had successes doing what you intend to do. For instance, Fedex, the overnight package delivery company was able to create this unique selling point by looking at how the banking industry operated. The banks sent their cheques to their hubs overnight. Fred Smith of Fedex used this model to send out packages overnight, which enabled Fedex to become an instant world leader in getting packages to you when you needed it – fast.

What I have discovered is that business people and entrepreneurs are generally willing to help others. They have learnt the value of supporting others – which is a gift they have almost certainly received from others when they needed it. Don't reinvent the wheel if someone else has already done what you intend to do, and has done it successfully. Model their success to help you to achieve your own success far more quickly.

My overriding determination and ambition helped me to push through the fear. I have felt the success in my bones for years but did nothing about it. This is definitely where I am meant to be.

I firmly believe that if we don't do what we are supposed to do when we are supposed to do it, the universe will create circumstances to force us to take action.

After my divorce, it seemed like all hell had let loose. It was as if everything that could go wrong, did go wrong. I had a fire in my shed whilst I was at work; one of my cousins and my grandfather passed away the same year; things were getting from bad to worse at work which resulted in me going on long-term sick leave for over a year and the following year my youngest of four elder brothers died.

The fire in my shed a few months after my divorce was almost the signal of things to come. I was at work in the middle of a training course when I was given the news that I had a fire at home. After giving my apologies to the course participants, I raced home to find that the fire was only in my shed. The fire fighters suspected that the hot sun had ignited tins of paint or related toxic substances. I was feeling very relieved that the children and I still had a home and a roof over our heads to come home to.

I spent my formative years growing up with my grandfather in Jamaica. My children and I had spent the previous Christmas with him before he passed away. This was the same Christmas that my divorce absolute had been finalised. It felt very fitting for us to spend this time with my grandfather, whom I loved very dearly like a father. The news of his death hit me pretty hard. Although it was only six months since I last saw him, and I had spent all my spare money on our holiday to visit him and the rest of the family in Jamaica, I knew that somehow I just had to see him one last time to say goodbye. I asked family and friends to lend me enough money for the flight and just enough to keep me going for the two weeks I was there. I was barely able to contribute any money to funeral expenses, but

I overlooked this because my priority was to take time out to honour a great, loving man – my grandfather.

Asking for help then was very new to me and it was something I was still uncomfortable with. My philosophy regarding money at the time and even now is if I haven't got the money to buy something that I want, I won't buy it. It has to be a very, very good reason for me to use a credit card or take out a loan. For instance, I only ever use my credit card to pay for holidays if I know that the money is in my bank to pay back the credit card straight away. I didn't even have a credit card at the time of my divorce and my grandfather's death. On this occasion however, I would have done almost anything to get the money to be able to honour my grandfather.

Just around the same time as my divorce decree nisi, I had applied for and got a new position in another Department within the organisation. I was feeling particularly pleased about it because it involved training and developing people, something that I loved to do. I had my welcome letter from my new manager, together with my new starters information. Within a couple weeks of starting my new job, I received a letter from personnel highlighting my employment details, terms and conditions of employment, including my contract of employment. The contract clearly stated that my position was a temporary one. It was a fixed termed contract. This was the first I was made aware of this and all the previous documentation I received had omitted this one important factor. When I checked with my manager about the temporary nature of my position, he seemed surprised and said:

"Bloody hell! They've only gone and sent you the draft job description and person specification!"

My personnel colleague from the previous Department who was involved in my transfer to the new Department was also not made aware of the temporary nature of my new position. I asked her if she would be willing to write me a testimonial to this effect. This she did, but to no avail. I spent the rest of my time in that particular Department contesting the temporary nature of my job, and later on, requested a transfer to another training job, as this one had not met my needs or expectations. I was getting bored as the job provided very little stimulation and variety. The Department showed me neither courtesy, nor remorse and was rather dismissive of my situation and their role within it. Neither the written testimonial from my personnel colleague nor trade union intervention helped to rectify the situation. At this stage, I was feeling very relieved at being able to get away from the situation for my five weeks vacation to Jamaica. My work situation impacted on my health and well being and only added to increase my stress levels.

Nothing had changed on my return to work from my vacation. This and the above circumstances in my personal life culminated in me going on long-term sick leave absence. During this time, I asked for and seized the opportunity to see the Department's Employee Counsellor. Thankfully, she was very good and was able to stay ahead o f me during the process. She assisted me to come to terms with my personal and work-related situation.

> *"It doesn't matter how many times you fall down; what matters is how many times you get back up."*
> *Morris Goodman (The Miracle Man)*

My youngest of four elder brothers died suddenly towards the end of my long-term sick leave. The universe had partially prepared me for this. It was exactly a year after my grandfather's death. I had plucked up the courage to do a reading at my grandfather's funeral then. Although I had no experience of organising a funeral, the responsibility of organising my brother's funeral fell on my shoulders. Needless to say, that this extended my long-term sick leave absence.

On returning to work, I insisted that I be relocated into a different job. It resulted in several temporary placements, all of which epitomised the treatment I had received from that Department since joining them. After more frustration, sick leave and the Department mishandling my work situation, I ended up taking on the largest local authority in the UK single-handedly at an employment tribunal.

The legal system had experienced new changes at this time, which meant that all the solicitors that I had approached for help with my case were reluctant to represent me. I believed so strongly in my case that I continued anyway, with the help of a retired businessman Paddy Sterrett. I decided to stop when I lost my appeal on a technical point at the European

Court of Appeal. I still believe that this was the right thing for me to do. I was glad I had the strength and courage to pursue the case. My focus now was on my health and the need to move on with the rest of life and my business.

All the above experiences ended up being like a snowballing effect of what felt like the ultimate roller coaster ride of the century; a ride of highly emotionally charge experiences that I had ever had in the whole of my life.

Though I had lost my case, I satisfied myself with the knowledge of Karma, i.e. what goes around comes around. Since leaving the authority, I had had updates from time to time from colleagues I had stayed in touch with. Sure enough, those who had mistreated me were having similar treatment done unto them. Karma.

My horrible experiences which, lead me to eventually challenge my previous employer in an employment tribunal case, made me stronger. It forced me to continue to ask for help. It gave me the push to do what I was destined to do.

Though it was a very rough ride, I know that it is an experience that I needed to give me the push that I needed. To all my good, bad past and current experiences I say thank you.

> *"Success isn't how far you got, but the distance you travelled from where you started."*
> ***Anonymous***

People allow fear to consume them to the extent that they live their lives to please others. They fear rejection, criticism or failure. The result is that they end up being miserable and blame others for their situation. They are not taking control of their own lives. The damage that this causes to one's self esteem, self-image, ambition and desire to achieve is immense.

In order to be a successful entrepreneur, you need to be able to push through the fear and take risks. Failure is a necessary part of success. Life gives us challenges to learn from and to help us to grow. This is also true for your business. If you fall, pick yourself up, brush yourself off, learn from your mistakes and start again.

Be A Winner

Giving up was never an option for me, no matter how challenging my circumstances were as a new business start up. I didn't have a lot of business skills, I didn't understand many business concepts nor did I have a niche market.

I went on short business skills courses delivered by people who themselves were either employees or self-employed, but these didn't really tell me anything about the real business world. They told me I needed to do things like business planning and market research. Yes, these are important facets of a successful business; however, my experience along my business journey has taught me that it is essentially the Success Mindset Principle^{TM} that is so crucial to bring about my success. You can have your business plan and market research, but still not do anything with it if you do not have the right mindset and a desire to succeed.

For me the **Success Mindset Principle**™ includes:

- Self-belief
- Confidence
- Determination
- A huge desire to succeed
- Trusting and following your intuition
- Vision
- An inner knowing that you are a **WINNER**
- Focus on your primary aim in your life as a driving force.

I used most of my first two years of being in business working in the business world to 'work to learn'. Not having a niche market made my experience somewhat more difficult and from time to time this helped to knock my confidence. I wanted to get there fast, but it wasn't happening, which brought about a lot of impatience and frustration.

I spent time developing myself both personally and professionally. I spent thousands of pounds doing so. I can tell you that this has paid off. For me, on-going personal and professional development is so absolutely crucial for business success. Too many young businesses or new start-ups do not see this as important and do not invest time or money on themselves. Their main focus is on being a technician in their businesses and then they wonder why things are not happening for them or why they are not successful.

My business vision is still the same today as it was at the start of my business venture, except it has been fine tuned with new knowledge and skills gained over the years. The key concepts are still there. My core business services again are still the same except with a lot more clarity and experience added to them.

Over the years I have attempted to find the right niche market that I was happy with. None of them felt right. The main thing is to keep testing, to keep moving forward. I always knew that my niche would involve assisting people in their personal lives. It was just a case of carving out that particular market for myself that would give me that competitive edge. Not having a specific niche that I was happy with meant that I was getting work from wherever I could get it and especially to pay the bills. This is a very common experience for many business start-ups.

Throughout my journey I felt the fear and did it anyway. My huge desire to succeed kept me going together with using my life vision as my driving force. Part of my life vision and visualisation is focusing on the house I intend to have in the future. Along my journey to achieve this future goal, I see myself, in my mind, signing my various books at bookstores, enjoying myself on stage at large venues and relaxing in my swimming pool. It has worked for me and it will work for you too.

Keep Your Goals Confidential

Keep your goals totally confidential so that others won't get the opportunity to criticise or try to stop you from achieving them. Tell only those who are likely to support you. This is a point worth repeating several times. Sadly, too many people stop themselves from setting big goals because of what other people may say. They then live a life full of 'what might have been's' or 'what if's'.

Life is about balance. As you become more aware of who you are and what you have to offer, you'll find you relate to others better. Fear is a powerful energy that can either control you or be controlled by you. Use it and channel its energy into assisting you to get the positive things you want to have in your life and business.

"Duty does not require a person to submit to the destruction of his personal ambitions and the right to live his own life in his own way".
Napoleon Hill

Mind your own business! Make your plan to achieve your goals and stick with it. You'll find you can take responsibility for your actions and for your life. Let other people take responsibility for their own situations; don't worry about their problems. This will make you feel a whole heap lighter and more able to focus on where you are going. When you feel good about yourself, you make good choices about what you do, what you say and how you conduct your life and business. This is self-love. You can serve your family, friends and associates and still be the person you want to be and need to be in order for you to achieve your dream goals. The difference is that you set the agenda and parameters.

How Many Dormant Lizards Do You Have Lying Around?

One evening whilst on holiday abroad in Spain, my eldest son and his friend believed they spotted a lizard in the night near the hotel. They were convinced it was a lizard. The next morning they went back to check if it was still there. To their surprise it was not a lizard after all, but a piece of stick.

I can tell you that they were a lot more relaxed on discovering that the 'lizard' was in fact a piece of stick. Had they not gone back to check, they probably would have lived the rest of their lives believing that Spain was a country they would not want to visit again because it had lizards.

So, go back and check your fears again. How real are they now? How many dormant lizards do you have lying around?

"When I look back on all the worries, I remember the story of the old man who said on his deathbed that he had a lot of trouble in his life, most of which never happened."
Winston Churchill

We all worry unnecessarily. I know it is something I have been particularly bad at in the past. We can never eradicate fear from our lives totally because there will always be a situation to challenge us, however, it's what we do about the fear that matters.

Remember that, if you are feeling anxious about a new situation, everyone else in that new situation will be feeling pretty similar. Leo Sayer, pop singer in the 70's and 80's used to be violently sick every time he was due to perform. This was an indication of his adrenaline rush and he usually ensured he used it to give his best performance every time.

Napoleon Hill, in his book '*Think and Grow Rich*', identifies six basic fears from which all other fear elements originate. These are:

Fear of poverty

Fear of criticism

Fear of ill health

Fear of the loss of love of someone

Fear of old age

Fear of death.

He reveals that fear is ultimately a state of mind and nothing else. So the majority of our fear is not real, unless, of course, you are faced with a real life dangerous situation that you need to deal with.

Unconsciously we often create situations and circumstances in our lives which prevent us from taking action. We lie to ourselves and pretend we don't know or that we can't do certain things. We make excuses or as T.D. Jakes says 'ex-cues.'

However, inevitably the idea or dream that you have been putting off will keep coming back to you time and time again until it almost stops you in your tracks until you do something about it. The truth is, no one else can do it like you can. No one else sees it the way you do.

When is now!

You were destined to be great! However, you may have convinced yourself otherwise.

> *"The trouble with most people is that they think with their hopes or fears or wishes rather than with their minds".*
> **Lady Nancy Astor**

Avoidance

When you allow fear to take over, you go into avoidance mode which means that you react to anything that is thrown at you instead of responding. You make less effective choices.

The only way out of fear is through it. How long will you allow yourself to be held back? You need to know that, no matter what, you can handle whatever you are faced with. Taking hold of fear and using it to help you lets you respond at a far higher level.

Ask high quality questions – who, when, where, how, what?

Use the resources you have around you. If you are not aware of the resources you have around you, get help to identify them. We usually have so many untapped resources around us. I have found family, friends and associates valuable resources who offer insights I may have overlooked on my journey.

So what does fear represent for you?

- What triggers off your fear?
- What does it look like?
- Who do you hear?
- What does it feel like?
- What do you hear?
- Where in your body do you feel the fear?
- Where did the fear originally come from?

> ***"Lord make me so uncomfortable that I do the very thing that I fear"***
> ***Ruby Dee***

Here are some ways of stopping fear preventing you from being the entrepreneur you want to be:

- Get rid of It!
- Take the risk
- Move out of your comfort zone
- Decide and do it! Take action
- Be honest with yourself and others
- Learn to trust yourself. Follow your intuition and your first thought.

- Positive self talk
- Read Jennifer McLeod's "Fear Not! 72 Ways to Eliminate Fear" inspirational pocket booklet
- Identify the cost and the benefits of you staying in that particular situation.
- Take responsibility for yourself and your actions.
- Acknowledge the truth that no one else can do what you do like you do. No one else has your unique talents and abilities.
- Identify your UNIQUE YOU and flaunt it!
- Ask yourself power questions or high quality questions.

What do you now believe about yourself?

Which underlying beliefs are fuelling your fire?

What are the driving forces in your life?

Successful Entrepreneurs

Successful people see themselves as self-development projects. They are constantly developing themselves and research shows that they spend an absolute minimum of £12,000 per annum on their personal and professional development. Things we do on a regular basis become habits. Habits are things that can be changed. They are not you and are separate from you. It will take you approximately between 21-30 days to change a habit if you choose to do so.

Ted Nicholas, often known as the 'Entrepreneur's Entrepreneur', has earned as much as $1,000,000 from a single ad. In his book '*Turn Words into Money*' he says that, in order to be more successful, you need to increase your failure rate!

Though he is highly successful, he acknowledges that it is having 4 or 5 times more failures than successes that have given him the successes that he now enjoys. Conversely, he believes that it is the fear of success that mainly stops people from starting a business, as opposed to fear of failure.

For me, I believe both fear of failure and fear of success contributed to my initial slow progress. This was coupled with my mindset at the beginning of my journey when I was unable to sustain the bigger picture of what I saw and felt. I had to change! I had to change my thinking, which in turn changed my self-belief. This meant that I **could** achieve all of the big successes that I felt and envisaged. Now I am so very comfortable with the big picture and ready to take on board the success that is due to me and that I desire and deserve.

"The way to develop self confidence is to do the thing you fear and get a record of successful experiences behind you. Destiny is not a matter of chance, it is a matter of choice; it is not a thing to be waited for, it is a thing to be achieved."
William Jennings Bryant

The seed to your destiny is already planted within you. You just need to take time to look for it. Identify what makes you tick.

- What inspires you?

- Who inspires you?
- What sets your heart on fire every time you think of it?
- What makes your heart sing?

Whatever it is, do it.

When you take responsibility for your life, you begin to take action. Taking responsibility for what you do and the results of your actions increases your self-value. This helps you to feel good about yourself and what you do.

Life is about choices. What will you do now? Continue to let fear keep its grip on you, or push through the fear and do it anyway?

There is one thing that we all definitely have total control over and that is our mind and the thoughts we choose to feed it. In order for you to be successful and rich, you must feel good about yourself and have very high self-esteem. Go to work on you today.

> *"He who is not everyday conquering some fear has not learned the secret of life"*
> *Ralph Waldo Emerson*

Releasing The Fear Exercise

Think of a situation that you are feeling fearful or anxious about.

Take several deep breaths, breathing from your abdomen.

As you breathe in, your abdomen should expand. As you breathe out, deflate your abdomen. (This is the correct way to breathe. If you are not used to breathing this way, take time to get used to it).

Acknowledge that the fear is there. Acknowledge and notice that the fear itself is not you – it is a *feeling* that YOU are having or experiencing and, therefore, is separate from you. Allow it to be there.

Then ask yourself: Is it possible that you could let go of the fear? Would you let go of the fear? If you are not willing to let go of the fear now, when will you let it go? In five minutes? Three hours? Tomorrow? If you are willing to let go of the fear, when will you let it go? Then let go of the fear. Release the fear. Decide you no longer have any use for it and let it go.

Now take a few more deep breaths. Acknowledge to yourself how much of the fear is left. Allow it to be there. Acknowledge it is ok for it to be there. Again, ask yourself: is it possible for you to let go of the fear? Would you let go of the fear? Are you willing to let go of the fear? When will you let go of the fear? Let go of the fear.

If there is any fear remaining, repeat this cycle until all the fear relating to the situation has disappeared. Congratulate yourself. Notice how you are feeling right now. Feel your courage and know that you deserve to be more, do more and have more.

Well done!

This is a useful exercise for releasing any emotion that is holding you back and that is unhealthy for you. It is often referred to as the Sedona method, however, it is a process that I have been using personally for years for my own development without knowing that it had such a name.

> *"Character cannot be developed in ease and quiet. Only through experience of trial and suffering can the soul be strengthened, ambition inspired and success achieved."*
> *Helen Keller*

Now connect with your inner child, the little **YOU** within. See the little you at the age of three or four or as close to this age as possible. You will make this connection better when you focus on your centre, the mid-section located just beneath your navel.

When you focus your attention and energy on this section, you will notice a warm sensation after a little while. It is at this point that you may notice the difference in your experience. Tell the little You how much you love them. Tell them whatever they need to hear you say. Show them all the love you possibly can and increase the love some more.

What would you have wanted to hear when you were that age? Tell them.

You are now in control.

Before you leave them, reassure them you will always be there for them no matter what and that you will be back again soon.

Connecting with your inner child on a daily basis is a very useful tool to increase your self-love and self-confidence.

Below is a useful poem that you can use to remind yourself of who you are.

'I'm Special …

In all the world there's nobody like me; nobody has my smile;

Nobody has my eyes, nose, hair or voice;

I'm Special …

No-one laughs like me or cries like me; no one sees things just as I do; no one reacts just as I would react.

I'm Special …

I'm the only one in all creation who has my set of abilities. My unique combination of gifts, talents and abilities are an original symphony

I'm Special …

I'm rare; and in all rarity there is great value;

I need not imitate others, I will accept – yes, celebrate – my DIFFERENCE

I'm Special …

And I'm beginning to see that God made me special for a very special purpose.

God has a job for me that no one else can do as well as I do.

Out of all the applicants only one is qualified. That one is me.

Jennifer McLeod

Because …I'm Special!'

Anonymous

> ### How You Can Use This Chapter To Empower Yourself:

- Choose to take action

- Decide if you want to succeed in your business and in your life

- Identify the steps you will need to take in order to push through your fear

- Take the risk! Being in business is about taking calculated risks

- Take responsibility for your actions and inactions and the results they bring.

- Become aware of when you are allowing fear to hold you back. And do something about it.

Chapter 4
Secrets Of Dynamic Goal Achievement That Will Take You To The Stars And Beyond.

"You are, at this moment, standing, right in the middle of your own acres of diamonds."
Earl Nightingale

In chapter One on The Power of Belief we looked at Be, Do and Have as the process necessary to achieve what you want in life. That same process applies here.

My Formula for Success when applied will also take you much further along your journey than you otherwise might have been.

The absolute number one requirement for goal achievement is to always keep your eye on the bigger picture. Imagine it, feel it, touch it and use all your senses to have the experience of achieving the goal NOW. It's important to think about this as an already achieved goal. This will help you to realise the goal and enjoy the truly fantastic experience that it will bring you.

Much has been written about goal setting over the years. The important focal point for me is the emphasis here on goal *achievement*. This keeps you focused on how you will achieve the goals once you have set them. It also goes a long way to develop and maintain your motivation – this is essential for goal achievement.

> *"Learn from the past, set vivid, detailed goals for the future, and live in the only moment of time over which you have any control: now."*
> *Denis Waitley*

Have BIG DREAMS and BIG GOALS. Create energy around yourself by actively working towards achieving your dream goals. Inactivity will never make it happen.

Inside-Out Approach

'*Think and Grow Rich*' was a wise title chosen by Napoleon Hill, for he knew the importance of first having the goal in your mind and keeping it there until it materialises. Another key ingredient for dynamic goal achievement is, as Napoleon Hill suggests, attaching as much emotion as possible to achieving your goal. The energy and emotion associated with acquiring your goal will help you to get there much faster. It will also give you a great sense of having already achieved your goal. The process enables you to apply all of your senses to achieving your goals.

> *"The price of success is hard work, dedication to the job at hand, and the determination that whether we win or lose, we have applied the best of ourselves to the task."*
> *Vince Lombardi, American football coach*

Programme your mind into believing that you already have that goal. Pretend you have that goal now. Write down the goal, repeat it regularly each day and visualise yourself experiencing that goal.

Each day, first thing on rising, I visualise my life vision, part of which includes a house. I go to different rooms in the house in my mind and even areas surrounding the house. The more feeling and positive emotion you attach to your goal, the quicker it will manifest itself for you. Stick with it.

Give yourself a definite date when you will achieve your goal.

How will you know you have achieved it?

How will you measure your achievement?

To ensure that your goal is not just something on your wish list or just a task, ask yourself:

What will this goal give me?

What are my reasons for wanting this goal?

What will I get that I don't already have in my life right now?

In a lot of cases the true answer will be an intangible one such as peace of mind, tranquillity, harmony, certainty or quality time for yourself and family. If your goal is to have financial abundance, what will that give you that you don't have in your life right now?

For instance, long before I had my current home, I had written a description of the house at least two to three years beforehand. When I found it, it was pretty much exactly has I had written it down. Only two things did not match my original list. However, it did not matter and certainly does not detract from the beautiful home I have right now. The décor, the spaciousness, the kitchen, the garden full of flowers – everything as I had described it and visualised it.

"You may have a fresh start any moment you choose, for this thing that we call 'Failure' is not the falling down, but the staying down."
Mary Pickford

Keep Going

The crunch in real goal achievement boils down to how much you really want to achieve that goal and what your reason or purpose is for wanting that goal.

With a strong sense of purpose behind you, you will be able to achieve anything you desire. It is your persistence, determination and hard work that will help you realise the goal that you are focusing on.

Once you have got your plan, commit yourself to making it happen. Never, ever give up. If your plan goes wrong then it is not the end of the world. You could say to yourself:

"OK, that didn't work! What can I do differently to change things?"

I also ask myself "What lessons can I learn from this situation?" Or

"What are the positives in this situation?"

I believe that there is at least one positive outcome within every negative situation. I have found this to be true from my own negative situations because I focused my mind on looking for the positive outcomes. For instance, the snowballing affect that happened right after my divorce. Whilst it was a most horrendous experience when it was happening, nevertheless, from time to time I would ask myself "What is actually good about my divorce?" For me, the answer were things like:

"I can do what I really want to do"

"I can really be me now!"

"I don't have to pretend that I am less than what I was meant to be."

"I can really go to work 'on' me now in earnest."

"The sky is the limit!"

Even when my grandfather died, I still managed to find lessons to learn from or positive outcomes. I can here you asking, "How can there ever be a positive outcome from someone dying?"

I was asked by one of my aunts to do a reading from the bible at the funeral. I was 'dying' inside and wanted to say no because of fear of failure and fear of others seeing the 'real me'. The 'real me' that would probably end up crying throughout the whole of the reading. Yes I did cry, mainly at the beginning of the reading, but I kept going anyway – for my grandfather, even though my voice was barely audible.

This situation forced me to push through the fear and to do what I needed to do in honour of my grandfather. It also helped me to see that it was ok to be me, and in front of so many people. Of all the many grandchildren, more than forty, I was the one chosen to do that reading. I was meant to do this.

As it happens, this was part of my preparation for what was to come the following year. My youngest elder brother in the UK died suddenly from brain haemorrhage. I was the only one able to lead and organize his funeral. My mum was totally distressed and unable to think straight to the point where she took her anxiety out on me (read more about our relationship in my forthcoming books); my sister took herself out of the picture as her way of dealing with his death; my parents were separated at this time and my dad was living somewhere else, and my other brothers were living in Jamaica. I knew very little about organizing a funeral, but I had to do it and get on with it. I cried as I read his eulogy, but it didn't matter. I had already had a similar experience at my grandfather's funeral, which I used to remind myself that it was ok and that I could do it.

If things don't go as you originally planned, at least then you will have had an experience and some more knowledge of what to do or in some cases what not to do. This is valuable information and needs be treated as such. If you fall down, pick yourself up, brush yourself off and start over again.

My fear of failure used to hold me back because of my cautious nature, however I had to learn to follow through with my plans no matter what once I had decided I was going to do something. In the end I asked myself 'What's the worst thing that can happen with this plan, idea or goal?'

Do not allow fear to stop you from formulating a plan of action and following through 'in case it goes wrong'.

I cannot emphasise enough how crucial this last step is and is definitely worth repeating several times. Too many small businesses and new entrepreneurs give up at the first hurdle. If all babies gave up every time they fell over, the majority of us would still be crawling today. Start believing you have achieved your goal and open your mind to the greater possibilities coming your way.

> *"My philosophy is that not only are you responsible for your life, but doing the best at this moment puts you in the best place for the next moment."*
> *Oprah Winfrey*

People like Henry Ford, Walt Disney, Oprah Winfrey, Sylvestor Stallone and Arthur Ashe would not have achieved their successes if they did not have that self-belief and determination to keep going.

Everyone told Henry Ford that the model car he wanted could not be made. One year later he got his dream car.

Sylvestor Stallone ended up producing his own films, as all the producers he approached thought he was a joke; and the rest is history.

To date, less than a handful of people know my major life vision. Keep your goals absolutely confidential and only share them with people who are likely to say 'Yes' and support you in your achievement.

Skills And Attitude

Identify the skills, knowledge and attitude you need to achieve that goal. If you haven't got them, then make a plan to get them.

At the beginning of my business development I completed at least four short certificated courses at the same time as completing my degree in psychology. Once my academic study was out of the way (at least for the time being) I then began to study my business. I don't say this to impress you but to impress upon you the need for ongoing personal and professional development.

One of the important factors in business is to know the state of your finances and manage them effectively. This was definitely one of the business areas that I needed to improve on and I set about systematically improving my knowledge and understanding of this area.

You need to be honest with yourself and admit any weaker areas that you can improve on. Make a plan to develop yourself personally and professionally. Your business success depends on it.

If, however, there are certain specialist skills that you do not possess which are necessary for the development of your business, then bring in people with these skills; skills that complement yours.

> *'Before you can do something, you first must be something'*
> **Goethe**

Once you have decided on your goal(s), ensure that they are challenging and stretch you. If you need to move your deadline in order to achieve your goal then do so. This is exactly what I have done in order to ensure that I achieve my vast life vision. If your goal is not challenging, it is not a goal and certainly will not keep you motivated.

Your True Goals

"If you don't know where you are going, it doesn't matter which way you go"
Cheshire Cat in Alice in Wonderland.

- What goals do you have to develop a better relationship with yourself?

- Where are you taking your life?

- What do you feel or believe is your real purpose on earth?

- Whatever your purpose in life is, align all other goals with your life purpose.

Michael Gerber in *E Myth Revisited* refers to your life vision as your primary aim in your life. What is yours? Be true to yourself.

Being clear about your personal values in your life will help you to identify your goals for achievement. The goals must be in alignment with your values. I highly recommend Stephen Covey's "*The 7 Habits of Highly Effective People*" as a fantastic source that covers values and mission statements in detail to enable you to achieve your goals.

> *"The mass of men lead lives of quiet desperation. What is called resignation is confirmed desperation."*
> *Thoreau*

So What IS The Magic Formula For Dynamic Goal Achievement?

There is no magic really, other than achieving your goals using an 'inside-out' approach and taking action. For instance, what will your goal look like? What will it feel like? It is simply doing what the great leaders have done to enable them to be successful and following their formulae exactly.

In summary, the process I use for achieving my goals is:

GOAL	Reason/ What will it give me?	Date	How will I Achieve it?	Who can help me?	Where? i.e. place or country	£ Cost?	How will I know I have achieved it? What will it look and feel like?

This process also embraces the SMARTER elements of goal achievement, whereby the goal is:

Specific

Measurable

Achievable

Realistic

Timebound

Evaluated

Reviewed.

I break the goal down into manageable chunks and separate sub-headings (How will I achieve it?) with separate deadlines for achieving each chunk always working towards the overall deadline for achieving the bigger goal.

Now over to you!

How You Can Use This Chapter To Help You To Reach The Stars:

- Identify your life values
- Make a plan of action to regularly visualise your goals
- Identify who can help you to achieve your goals
- Ensure your goals are in alignment with your values
- Keep your goals confidential.

Chapter 5
How To Energise Your Mind, Body And Spirit

"Self love is the personal commitment to slowing down enough to embrace stillness, healing and renewal as a daily part of your own life. It also means nurturing and enriching every part of the self: mind, body and spirit. Self caretaking is how you embrace and incorporate the care of the mind, body and spirit into your being and daily life ritual. Self caretaking is created twice; first on the inside and then on the outside."
Toby Thompkins

Self-love will set you free. True self-love is a positive internal experience enabling your true authentic self to come to the fore. This has a positive effect on others around you. Self-love is not being conceited. Being conceited is a negative experience where you believe that you are better than everyone else. This has a negative effect on others around you

Your Body

Simply put, without you there is no business, unless of course you have been successful in developing systems for your employees to take over and run the business the way you originally intended it to be operated.

That is why it is so crucial for you to look after yourself each and every day.

Find your passion. Your passion will keep you energised and motivated.

Recognise your body's natural rhythms and patterns. Through yoga I have learnt that our physical body operates on a two and a half hour cycle throughout the day and night. Its rhythm speeds up and slows down to provide us with a balance of energies.

Take a break. Your mind and body will naturally slump mid-afternoon. Taking a 15-20 minute break or closing your eyes and ears for a few moments will give your mind and body that much needed re-charge. This will help you to be more effective and more efficient for the rest of the day.

Dr Gillian McKeith, author of *'You Are What You Eat'*, suggests eating living foods every day. This includes seeds, raw fruits and vegetables, essential fatty acids together with superfoods like barley grass to keep you healthy and give you the vitality you need.

> *"Living foods are enzyme powerhouses. By eating them you help maintain your own enzyme reserves and can more easily eliminate toxins, rejuvenate your cells and strengthen your system. Living foods help nourish brain cells, boost concentration and render clear thinking."*
> ***Dr Gillian McKeith***

Drinking plenty of water each day helps to keep your energy level in peak condition as well as providing the hydration that the body needs. An average of two litres of water is recommended for optimum health.

Rejuvenate your body with an exercise regime on a daily basis or at least three times for the week. I go with the flow of my body, especially my joints, to dictate what form of exercise or combination of exercises it wants on any particular day. I find exercising first thing in the morning helps me to start my day feeling energised, fresh and rearing to go. Your body is unique to you and will tell you what it needs to be at its best for you.

How we think we feel has an effect on how we actually feel physically. Your muscles will accept whatever your mind tells them.

Your Mind

What you think about you bring about. Keep your focus on what you want to have and not on what you don't want to happen. Do whatever helps you to feel replenished and energised. Whatever you see in your outer world is a direct result of what is going on in your inner world, in your head, albeit on a subconscious level.

Tony Robbins', the world's leading motivational speaker, success triad incorporates physiology, language and focus in order to change your state. That is to say that when you change what you say, change what you are focusing on and move or take action, your state changes as a direct result. You feel different, think differently and are able to see things from a different perspective, not to mention the increased surge of energy that you will attain by doing so.

> *"What if nothing around you holds any power to make you unhappy."*
> *Alan Cohen*

Awaken Your Intuition

We are all naturally intuitive beings, however, Western society places more emphasis on logic and on what can be scientifically proven. Intuition is neither logic nor intelligence. It is what enables you to be the REAL YOU, your true, authentic self. Intuition is an inner knowing, sometimes referred to as the 'sixth sense.'

Developing intuition is a process that will take time, especially if it is something that you are not used to. It emanates from the right side of your brain, your creative side and is not based on others telling you what to do.

Using your Intuition will be a different experience and feeling from anyone else's experience of their intuitive self. What feels, looks and sounds right for you may not be right for anyone else. It is a process that embraces all of your senses, if you allow it to do so. Give yourself permission to have this truly, beautiful, serene, rich, peaceful experience that is rightfully yours. This is and can be the result when you allow yourself to have this experience. I am much calmer and more at peace now as a result of having learnt to followed by intuition. Yes, meditation does have a role to play in developing your intuition also.

I had an experience with my youngest son's school. His existing school at the time had tried very hard to label him as having 'behavioral problems' and was taking drastic measures to solve very low-level behaviour situations that he and other children exhibited, such as shouting out the answers in class. To quote his class teacher: "He always wants to answer all the questions." He and the other bright children in the class were bored. Instead of the school recognizing this and acting on it appropriately, they chose to treat my son and the other bright children as the 'problem.' The acting head teacher was unfortunately not a man to be reasoned with. The result was that I made the decision to remove my son, Nathaniel, from that particular school.

One day I took the day off work and kept Nathaniel off school, so that we could visit a few schools that had places for his age group. At one of the schools that we visited, I could tell instantly by intuition that it was not a school for me before we even had a chance to look around. The secretary, who was very nice to me on the phone, was somewhat aloof towards me in person and it seemed as if she didn't quite expect me to be the person that she had been speaking to on the phone. There was no synergy between the head teacher and I either.

I tried to explain to Nathaniel why he wouldn't be going to that school, but he didn't quite understand. That school was his first choice, although he wasn't able to tell me why he preferred it over and above other schools that we looked at. For these reasons, I decided to go for another visit to this school and the school that his dad and I preferred, to help put all of our minds at rest.

When I rang the head teacher of Nathaniel's preferred school about a second visit, she said she had already spoken to the acting head teacher of Nathaniel's existing school. On the basis of what he had told her, she had decided that Nathaniel could only have a place at her school if his transfer was managed, i.e. if he transferred with the assistance of the education system's behaviour support team. Needless to say that I didn't accept her offer and told her that she had judged my son without even knowing him.

Follow your intuition; it will make all the difference to your life and your business.

Do not attempt to rationalise what your intuition reveals to you or what you feel. Ask and listen to your subconscious mind. It already knows the answers you seek

Don't TRY to access your intuition. Trying takes conscious, mental energy and will prevent you from doing so. Instead, let go, relax and allow yourself to have the experience

Trust in your instincts. If you are faced with a choice between two decisions, both of which may be attractive, let your intuition guide you. I allow my body to talk to me when I might be feeling indecisive about something. For instance, I get physical sensations in my stomach. If the decision is right for me, then there is no movement in my stomach, however, if it is the wrong decision then I will generally get a sensation in my stomach to tell me so. Whatever my intuition says will always be the best thing for me to do or say.

Quieten your mind and relax. Allow your thoughts to flow, not paying any particular attention to any of them. The inspiration you seek will reveal itself to you.

> *"I simply know that I smell things, I feel situations and when the crowd is silent I understand what it silently says. And I say it with a voice, with proper words."*
> *Lech Walesa*

Deep breathing helps you to activate your intuitive, creative right brain, together with bringing about a sense of calmness and peace around you.

Breathing deeply and slowly from your left nostril will bring about a sense of calmness and composure. On the other hand, breathing solely from your right nostril energises and stimulates you. Less than two minutes of breathing from either nostril will bring about the desired balanced effect. The natural rhythm of your body alternates between your nostrils breathing patterns throughout the day to bring about a sense of balance to your mind and body.

The majority of people do not breathe correctly, for example they do shallow breathing instead of breathing deeply using the stomach muscles and diaphragm. Taking a deep, long breath enables the diaphragm, located just under the rib cage, to work properly. The breath moves up to your chest area as you lift up on your rib cage. The deep breath fills the lungs and allows more oxygen to get to the brain, thus giving you more brain power.

Your Spirit

"The sense of rest that results from a practice of complete silence is a therapy of utmost value."
Norman Vincent Peale

Stand Still. Once in a while I have stood absolutely still on my journey, after all the hustle and bustle of the business world and sometimes frantic energy of attempting to get customers and direction. By standing still, I mean being still; being at one with yourself and the universe; being silent and taking time out in solitude. For instance if you find yourself on a plateau, seize the opportunity to take time out to connect with your inner spirit, your inner knowing for the answers you need to get off that particular plateau. Or if you find yourself getting confused or going nowhere fast, take time out. You will find that the very act of taking time out to connect with your inner spirit will enable you to get where you want to go far quicker than continuing in a state of confusion or frenzy.

Once I have stood still for as long as it takes, the answers begin to come my way. This is my opportunity to allow my intuition to guide me and for me to connect my spirit, my inner being to the universal life force energy.

Alternatively, stop, step back and take a bird's eye view of your situation in your business or life. Take a third person's objective position and look at your situation from the point of view of 'How did I get here?' and 'What would I need to do to get past this stage?'

"They died with all their music in them."
Oliver Wendell Holmes

Standing still is separate from and in addition to the practice of being still on a daily basis. Just a few minutes of stillness each day, as and when it is required, makes a huge difference to peace of mind and clarity. Allow yourself to receive the intuition that is readily available to you each and every day. It is another way of being totally refreshed to help you continue with your daily activities.

Being silent will give you the answers to your questions, as well as answers to questions you didn't know you had. Both your silence and standing still will enable you to tap into the universal energy force.

10 TOP TIPS that you could use to receive your gifts from the universe:

1. Sit down and sit still in total solitude for a minimum of 5 minutes with nothing or anyone to disturb you. Allow the inspirations to flow to your conscious mind. Don't attempt to rationalise any of the ideas you get from this experience. Accept them.

2. Write down the ideas you get last thing at night just before you go to sleep. Your mind is in a deep sense of relaxation at this time, which means you are more susceptible to receiving inspirations. This is also very useful if you suffer from insomnia.

3. Keep a pen and notepad readily available at the side of your bed for capturing your thoughts and ideas.

4. Write down your dreams exactly as you remember them. Each dream is likely to be a piece of the jigsaw puzzle in your life or business. Over a period of time, the jigsaw

puzzle will come together to give you the solution to a situation.

5. Make a mental and written note of the very first thought that you get on waking up in the morning. This first thought is likely to be the solution you needed for a situation. Take action to follow through with that first thought and make it a priority action point that same day. Remember that just picking up the phone or just diarising the activity is action in itself and is also a sign of your commitment to follow through.

6. Surrender. Don't push against the grain. If it's going to happen it will happen

7. Trust yourself. Trust that you are enough and that you do not need to go out of your way to prove yourself to others.

8. Stop for just a second throughout the day to send out positive thoughts to others and for others to receive success and happiness. The more you give out the more you will get back. Give gratitude for what you do have

9. Your body's natural rhythms usually slow down in the afternoon. Take an afternoon break. This can be for as little as five minutes to allow your body to rejuvenate sufficiently in order to provide you energy for the rest of the day's activities.

10. Kundalini Yoga is fantastic for calming your mind, body and spirit in accordance with the universe's natural life force energies. Why not give it a try?

"You only lose energy when life becomes dull in your mind. Your mind gets bored and therefore tired doing nothing. Get interested in something. Throw yourself

*into it with abandon. Get out of yourself. Be somebody.
…..Getting into good causes… the more you lose yourself
into something bigger than yourself, the more energy you
will have. You don't have time to think about yourself
and get bogged down in your emotional difficulties."*
Norman Vincent Peale

Be like a child again. Allow yourself to play.

- When was the last time you did something spontaneous?

- What is it that you love to do?

- What activities give you the most pleasure?

- Who do you love?

- What do you value?

- What is your major contribution in this world?

- What legacy do you want to leave behind after you have left this world?

Have fun in your life. Not only do you feel good as a result of it, it also stimulates your creative right brain to give you even more ideas to help you in your life and business.

Focus on happiness rather than pleasure. Pleasure is a form of immediate self-gratification. Happiness, on the other hand, is a long-term goal; a long term journey to sheer joy, fulfillment and freedom. This is what you deserve. It is your right, and, it stimulates mind, body and spirit simultaneously.

Exercise:

On a scale of 1 – 10, (10 being high), where are you in your life right now in the areas of fun, fulfillment and freedom? Be honest with yourself. It is only when you are honest with yourself and acknowledge where you are at that you can move forward.

Where do you want to be in these areas in 12 months, 5 years or 10 years?

What steps do you need to take to fill the gap between where you are at now and where you want to be?

Then take action today towards making that a reality. It does not matter how small the action is as long as you do something. This is your way of showing commitment to making a difference in your life.

> **How You Can Use This Chapter To Stimulate Or Energise Your Mind, Body and Spirit:**

- Decide on an exercise regime that is comfortable and manageable for you, if you do not already have one. Start to exercise today

- Practice sitting still and in total solitude each day

- Expect to receive inspirations from the universe. As you follow through with the inspirations you receive from the universe, the universe will reward you by giving you more inspirations to take your life and business forward.

- Start to recognize and practice following your first thought

- Take up Kundalini Yoga.
- Practice deep breathing using your stomach muscles and your diaphragm.

Chapter 6
Secrets Of The Entrepreneur's Dream

"Success is going from failure to failure with great enthusiasm."
Mark Twain

What is the entrepreneur's dream? Simply put, it is anything you want it to be. Nothing magical or mystical, just that! You are in control; decide what you want to achieve and just go for it. Sounds simple doesn't it? It is. But simple doesn't mean it's easy. Whatever you want in life, you must be committed to working both hard and smart for it.

I remember when I started my first temporary job for a large local authority, when I was just nineteen. I'd had a couple of other temporary jobs, including a position as a Saturday Sales Assistant. The temporary job was a stepping-stone for me to get a foothold into the organization. After three months I had found and been appointed to a permanent position. I recall my manager saying at my leaving celebration, "I'm surprised you are going?"

"Well, you knew I would be leaving at some point given that it is a temporary contract", I replied

"Yeh, but not so quick!" he said.

Soon after starting my first permanent job at the bottom of the ladder within the local authority, my new manager said, ""I wasn't going to appoint you."

In surprise I asked, "Why not?"

"Because I didn't think you would stick around", he said

I guess I was surprised again at his response, however, they clearly saw something in me that I wasn't that aware of at that time. Sure enough I was off again eight months later, being promoted to a higher position within the organization.

Whilst I recognize that I was always ambitious, I guess I didn't realize everyone could see it in me from such an early age. Even people that I grew up with are now telling me that they always knew I would grow up doing something good and big. Indeed I had major challenges later on from two of my managers in the organization because they felt threatened by me. Again, they could see clearly that I was more than I was being at that moment in time under their management. That aside, my managers feeling threatened by what they saw in me was more about their own insecurities as managers than anything that I had done.

Certainly a couple of years later in the organization I was feeling that I could be more and do more, even after having received more promotions.

Over the years I worked in earnest to release and get rid of childhood baggage from both school and home. I could see and begin to feel the layers being peeled away, a bit like peeling an onion one layer at a time.

It was at this time that my perception of myself and what I was feeling inside, began to merge. I began to really see what others had been seeing in me for so long. Even now, sometimes when talking to some close business associates, they look at me with that 'look'. My response is usually 'What?' as if to say 'What did I say?' or 'What did I do?' They usually respond by smiling or shaking their heads. Afterwards, I realize that that 'look' is the familiar look from the past when others saw in me more than I was being at that moment in time.

As my eldest son, Ricardo once said to me, "Mum, the only reason you are a businesswoman is because it is part of your destiny. No matter what you did in life, you would have ended up being a businesswoman."

I always felt that I was born to win! I was born to be a trailblazer. My company Step Up! International Ltd is the first and currently the only company in the UK to work solely and specifically with separated and divorced women to help them rebuild their lives and create financial independence. There is no other company in the UK like it.

So I always had the winning streaks within me from an early age. All that was left for me to do was to begin to be and act the winner I was born to be.

> *"I haven't even started yet."*
> *Marianne Williamson*

My ABCD & KP Success Formula© 2006 is something that I developed to move me forward in achieving my own dream goals. It works - try it for yourself and see the benefits. However, in order to benefit from the formula, there must be a paradigm shift in your own mind. You need to be able to accept and be comfortable with your dream; you must believe it for it to become true for you.

It's important to actively and constantly develop yourself personally and professionally. Without this any big dreams that you want to achieve may not happen, because you may not have the capability to sustain them, even if you do achieve them.

Always be ready to receive and accept your inspiration. I got my inspiration for my Success Formula shortly after landing on my first plateau.

I remember I was visiting my mother in London who was sick at the time. It was the Christmas week and I was out and about running some errands for her. Whilst I was out walking and feeling good with myself about being able to spend this time with my mother, the Success Formula came to me. Just like that – out of the blue!

You can imagine I was smiling like a Cheshire cat. I wanted to run, jump and skip along the pavement but made myself content with people just staring at me wondering what I was on! I couldn't contain myself though and phoned a friend straight away with my mobile to tell her that I had just been given my very own Success Formula. She was absolutely bouncing off the wall too. I accepted that if successful people could have their own success formulae, then so could I. The only difference between them and myself was that they were further ahead in the business world than I.

The result of having this inspiration led me to identifying my life vision and creating a five year Life Action Plan incorporating both personal and business goals. At the front of this Life Action Plan are:

My Life Vision

The Jennifer McLeod ABCD&KP Success Formula© 2006

I use this Life Action Plan as part of my ritual every morning to power up my mind, body and spirit. It helps me to keep my focus, increase my own self-belief in the Plan and keeps both my conscious and subconscious minds working to come up with the answers for me to put the Plan into effect. I use my Success Formula to guide me and especially for the courage to do and be bold enough to carry out the Plan.

Having the Life Action Plan, or any other plan for that matter, does not mean that I know how to do everything contained within the Plan. I still need to find the answers in order to take the right action to implement any of the specific goals in the Plan.

I am modeling on successful entrepreneurs in order to implement goals from my Life Action Plan. I review and edit the Plan as and when necessary. This in itself generates more ideas in terms of implementation of the Plan.

The big difference in my life now as a result my Success Formula is that some of the things I wanted to achieve in my personal life and business are now coming to fruition.

For instance, in my personal life, these include friends I am attracting into my life, the house I have now, and the better connection with my children and extended family, and actively doing and enjoying my hobbies.

In the business world, these include creating the right niche market, being an investor, being an author, completing my psychology degree and diploma in coaching, attracting the right business people and speaking engagements. It has taken a huge investment of time, energy and money in myself for this to happen. And, yes, failures along the way too. The journey is ongoing.

The message here really is the sky is the limit!   You can achieve anything you choose to do. You don't have to always know how to do it!

Be a winner!

> *"Make the most of yourself, for that is all there is of you."*
> *Ralph Waldo Emerson*

Start acting the winner you want to be now and surround yourself with winners.

I was playing a game of pool with my youngest son Nathaniel, then 9 years old, and we were nearing the end of the game where all I had to do was to pot the black ball. I thought I would be 'kind' to him (even though it was he and his eldest brother that taught me how to play pool!) and let him pot the black and his last ball too. His response totally amazed me!

"I don't play with quitters! When I had only the black ball to pot I still carried on!"

All I could do at the time was quickly reframe my thinking and re-affirm to him that he was right not to play with quitters and to always surround himself with winners.

WOW! I was gobsmacked! What a lesson to learn from one so young. Children can be your teachers if you take the time to stand back and appreciate what your children are really saying. You may be surprised at the many lessons that you can learn from your own or other children around you.

There are various strategies I have used to get me to where I am now. You will have your own preferences, and it is important for you to go along with the things that feel right for you.

However, finding the right strategies for you doesn't mean that the strategies will be easy or that you will necessarily feel comfortable with them because of their newness. As a business owner and entrepreneur you will need to breakthrough your comfort zone to take risks and try something new from time to time. It is this flexibility that will start you off on your path to achieving your success, together with the willingness and determination to do so. However, you don't have to do it alone. Get help.

Developing Your Creativity

Most highly successful people have, at some time or another, been inspired by flashes of inspiration to help them achieve their success. I have been actively developing the creative side of my brain (this is the right side; left side is logical) for some time now.

The right side generates sixth sense experiences or intuition. On reading Napoleon Hill's classic *Think and Grow Rich*, not only was I thoroughly inspired and even more motivated about my life plan, but also my creative imagination was clearly heightened. I am not sure if this was sheer coincidence or whether that was the stage I had reached on my journey. It was also at this time that I began to meet like-minded successful people, with whom I was able to share my beliefs regarding my spirituality.

Here are some ways of developing your creativity:

a) Imaginary Committee

This is a fantastic method to use to get in touch with your creative right brain. As I explained earlier, it is definitely a winner and an effective tool in terms of giving you solutions to situations that may have eluded you for a while.

To create your imaginary committee imagine your role models and picture them in your head sitting round a table with you. When you have a situation that you are not sure how to deal with you simply ask each of the committee members in turn how they would deal with the situation. Expect to get an answer!

This is far better an approach than asking someone else for an answer, as they will give you an answer as *they* see the situation through their own eyes and not through yours.

Role models can be anyone, for example famous people alive or dead, politicians, historical figures, modern day icons, celebrities, business people, family members or friends. Essentially, they are anyone whose opinion you respect, or who has achieved great things and whose experience and knowledge you would like to have access to. Anyone who can help you to clarify your thinking or someone who has already done something successfully that you want to do. It is not necessary for your role model or mentor to be in the same business sector as you.

b) Grounding Yourself

Grounding yourself brings you a feeling of peace, serenity and oneness with the universe, enabling you to tap into the vast array of abundance that awaits you. When the mind is calm, the ideas and inspirations will come to you.

Sit comfortably on a straight-backed chair with your feet firmly on the floor or lay on a bed. Take several deep breaths from the stomach and release the breaths slowly out through the mouth.

As you exhale, tell yourself relax. In your mind, talk to every muscle in your body from your head to your toe, telling it to relax. This is called autogenic conditioning and was well used by the East Germans years ago in preparation for their sporting activities because of its effectiveness and which lead to the East Germans' many successes in this arena.

> *"Nothing can bring you peace but yourself."*
> *Ralph Waldo Emerson*

See and feel yourself totally anchored to the earth. See a golden light travelling from the top of your head to the soles of your feet far down into the ground, then doing a U turn and back into the soles of your feet, leaving you totally rejuvenated and revitalised. Relax.

> *"The sense of rest that results from a practice of complete silence is a therapy of utmost value."*
> *Norman Vincent Peale*

Modelling

This is another of the secrets of achieving the Entrepreneur's dream. Actively find out what other successful people, your role models, are doing and ask your role models quality questions like:

What did you do to accomplish this?

What does doing this really mean to you?

What values do or did you have that supported your success?

What beliefs do you need to have in order to achieve that level of success?

Then model on their success; in other words, copy what they do. Use the exact formula that they use to get the same results. Ask yourself how their processes or principles can be transferred to what you do.

Do What You Love To Do

"Four things come not back – the spoken word, the sped arrow, the past life and the neglected opportunity."
Arabian Proverb.

Doing what you love to do will assist you in maintaining the motivation, enthusiasm, commitment and belief in your business and your product. If you do what you love to do it stops feeling like work – the motivation is simply there. People will also see your passion for what you love to do.

I love what I do and would do it for free. What stops me is the constant reminder that I am in business to make a profit as well as sharing what I know and love with others.

In a recent teleconference with Jay Abraham and Chet Holmes, Chet reiterated the need for you to be clear about the person you want to become and set about achieving that dream. This mirrors Napoleon Hill's suggestion to spend thirty minutes per day on developing the person you want to become.

All the sports people who were fortunate enough to be coached by famous American coach Vince Lombardi, left his stewardship to become successful business people in their own right as he had taught them all about the power of belief.

If you do what you love to do and believe in yourself enough, then anything is possible.

Mistakes

Allow yourself to make mistakes. This is a sure way of you moving ahead, providing you learn from your mistakes or get help to do so.

It is worth repeating again that successful achievers are only at the top because they have fallen over countless times but have picked themselves up, learnt from their mistakes and started over again.

One of my mistakes at the beginning of the business was not having a very clear picture of my niche market. This meant that my marketing and selling was a haphazard process. Not only was I not reaching my niche client group, I was not able to describe them and, therefore, did not know where to look for them.

After a while I decided I could either continue playing a hit and miss game or I could stop and start all over again by getting the clarity of the target audience and focus on them only as my niche market.

It took me about two years before I was very clear and specific about who or what my niche market was.

This was when the business really took off, as I was very focused on who they were and had lots of ideas as to how to access them.

I appreciate that as a new business, you may not always be clear about your market. Even if you are, there may be the need to just get out there and get some money coming in, no matter where from as long as your bills are paid. There are always better solutions around the corner. Fear prevents us from being patient and we often choose the most convenient of the current options, rather than waiting for the right one.

> *"Fears are educated into us and can, if we wish, be educated out."*
> *Karl Menninger*

When I finally identified my niche market, all my business plans and dreams just simply fell into place! My planning and preparation had paid off.

As I explained earlier, I would not be so certain now of which client group I want to work with if I had not fumbled around in the dark at the beginning. It also feels very good and just right. As Napoleon Hill says, 'start where you are right now and the answers you need will come to you'. The teachers I needed to push my business forward also came to me just when I needed them most.

The very fact that you had the business idea in the first place is nature's way of telling you that you can be a success. It's really about how much you want it and the price you are willing to pay to get it!

My dentist, one of my friend's sister, decided about twenty years ago that she wanted to become a dentist. At this time she had two small children. She had left school with little or no educational qualifications, however, once she had made the decision that that was the profession that she wanted to pursue, she set about finding out about what she needed to do to achieve that goal.

She went back to basics and completed a course of ordinary and advanced level qualifications before completing her degree. She persuaded the bank to give her the required loan to set up her dental practice straight after university. She is still my dentist now, not because she is my friend's sister, but because she is very good at what she does.

She paid the price of taking on and committing to a minimum of ten years of full time studying and continuing to manage her household as a single parent. The fact that she left school with little or no qualifications did not deter her.

> *'Luck is what happens when preparation meets opportunity'*
> *Henry Ford*

Time Is Of The Essence

Time is one of those things that when it is gone, it is gone and you cannot get it back. So often we allow others around us (family, friends, associates, team members) to steal our time.

Be available to people on your terms, at least where your time is concerned. Identify your time wasters – be honest with yourself.

For instance how often do you respond to emails each day or click on an email without having sufficient time to deal with it right there and then? I only open my emails when I know I have time to deal with them. I prioritise my emails and touch them once per day. How many hours could you really spend each day on your emails? I'm sure your answer would be something like more hours than you could afford. Develop systems and use them.

I had been invited recently to attend a presentation for an opportunity that I was told would help me to get to where I want to go. That is all the information that I was given and nothing else, despite attempts to gather more information. It was packaged as a full day event which 'won't cost you anything to attend just a minimal £10.' I was invited to lunch on the same day, before the event, with an opportunity to discuss the day's event in the evening. The package included being chauffeur driven there and back.

I accepted the invitation, however, declined the lunch invitation and the 'treat' of being chauffeur driven.

I didn't know what the opportunity was and I was very clear from the outset that I was not willing to spend a day of my time without more information. It may have turned out to be totally unsuitable for my needs. I ensured that if I needed to get away at any point during the presentation, I had the option to do so without feeling guilty about it.

The person who invited me to hear the opportunity was not too pleased with my approach; however, I created a win-win solution for both of us. A whole day of your life doing something that does not contribute to your bigger purpose is a very costly experience, and a waste of your time; depending on how much value you place on your life. In the end I gave my apologies and declined his offer, as I was not convinced that it would be a good use of my time.

As a young business it's important to understand the business world. You need to make new contacts, and choosing the right opportunities is part of the process of using your time more effectively.

In a teleconference Jay Abraham explained how you can use your time smarter to maximise every effort and decision you make in your business, giving you and your clients more benefits. .

Make Decisions

Make the decision, whatever it may be. Not making a decision leaves you in further indecision and on a path of procrastination. Making a decision to make the decision at a later identified date is itself making a decision. Successful business people make decisions fast and change them slowly.

"The most difficult things is the decision to act, the rest is merely tenacity. The fears are paper tigers. You can do anything you decide to do. You can act to change and

control your life and the procedure. The process is its own reward.
Robyn Davidson

Sacrifice

As an Entrepreneur you must be willing to make sacrifices to get to the top. How much do you want it and what price are you willing to pay to get it?

'Price' here can mean spending less time with your family, remortgaging your house, spending less time on hobbies, reduced hours of sleep or living on less money. Money certainly will be a major factor for any new business. Somehow you will need to get hold of extra finances to fund your business.

In my opinion there is a serious lack of real support for young businesses both financially and in other business aspects.

Doing all that you possibly can do to finance your business is absolutely imperative.

Have you approached family and friends?

Have you sought support through grants?

Have you approached your bank or other banks and building societies for a loan?

What assets do you have that could potentially provide a source of income for your business?

Do you own your own house?

Is there any equity available as a possible option of finance?

I had put aside funds to support my family and some financial capital I needed to enter into the business full-time. When the capital was depleted, my next option was to look at other methods of funding my business.

I obtained an initial business loan from my bank, which was quite a minimal sum in comparison with the ideas I had for my business. This was at a time when I was still feeling my way into the business and uncertain as to how much I would really need.

When this loan had finished and I had a better idea of what was really needed to expand my business, I was prepared to look at all possible options including releasing equity from my house to do so. I did use equity in my house to fund my business. It certainly made a big difference to the operation of my business, not to mention the reduction in my stress levels.

Mistakes with money are one of the many mistakes that young businesses make. Be willing to learn from them to push you forward.

I have had my challenges with lack of finance to develop my business; however, I explored every option of getting finance before ruling it out. Someone, somewhere, will loan you the money, even if the banks tell you no.

"It is hard to fail, but it is worse never to have tried to succeed. In this life we get nothing save by effort."
Theodore Roosevelt

Paying the price of spending less time with family as a new business owner is likely to be one of the many challenges you will be faced with. For me, this was one of my main challenges, as spending quality time with my family is embedded within my values. Whilst I accept that it has been a challenge, it can be achieved. For instance, I am an early riser so waking up earlier in the morning or working later at night around the family has worked for me.

The various facets of the business demand both time and energy. Going full out in terms of my own personal and professional development was part of the sacrifice I was prepared to make in terms of my readiness for the business world and becoming an expert in my field.

It can be easy to push hobbies to one side initially as a new business or young business, especially when challenged by time. I love singing, painting and dancing. Admittedly, over the years they have been squeezed out from time to time until I got myself back into a routine where I could schedule them into my routine. I now have several of my own paintings on display around the house.

Singing has always been one of my childhood ambitions. When I was about twelve years old, I told my mother that I wanted to be a singer. She suggested that I asked my music teacher at school for information about what I needed to do to become a singer. My music teacher said that he was willing to give me lessons at school. This happened for a little while, but didn't work out. Since then the child within me has been yearning to be that singer. Many,

many years after leaving school I had taken part in a musical produced by my local arts centre, in addition to searching for and taking part in short singing courses and sampling local non-conventional choirs. I have now managed to find the right local singing coach for me. He is very proficient at what he does and has a track record of working with high profile singers like Chaka Khan and Anita Baker. My singing ambition now is to be proficient as a singer so that I can pass on my knowledge and skills to disadvantaged children who otherwise may not get the opportunity.

Many successful entrepreneurs tend to be early risers, either by nature or design. If you are not, are you willing to do what is necessary for you to become one so that you can get more out of your day?

I welcome the early hours of the morning when the rest of the family are still asleep. This is my quiet time to meditate, do my affirmations, revisit my goals, do my exercise, read and generally power up my mind and body for the day's successes (or failures: generally known as lessons). This is my time to connect with my inner spirit.

Once you have decided on the sacrifice you will make, acknowledge and accept the consequences that will result from those sacrifices.

Accepting the consequences does not mean that you necessarily like them or are happy with them, it just means that you accept them and are prepared for them. Keeping your eye on the bigger picture will help you to remain focused and stop you complaining when things are tough!

"There is never time in the future in which we will work out our salvation. The challenge is in the moment; the time is always now".
James Baldwin

An article in Advice4Growth business journal revealed that half of entrepreneurs say "never again." The main reason was employment legislation, as entrepreneurs encountered red tape that made business very complicated. Taking on new employees also created a host of potential challenges to overcome.

On the other hand, 'nearly a quarter of would-be entrepreneurs in the West Midlands are failing to realise their dream due to a variety of fear factors.' The main barriers reported were 'risk of losing security' and 'fear of unknown day-to-day costs.' Again, how much do you want it and what price are you willing to pay?

"To fight fear, act. To increase fear – wait, put off, postpone."
David Joseph Schwartz

Motivation

Anyone who has survived the first two years of business will tell you that it is not easy. So many obstacles come your way and you have so many unknown things to deal with not to mention lack of finances. If you believe in yourself and in what you are doing you will find a way through it all.

I failed my 'A' level (Advanced Level) qualifications when I was eighteen which meant that I was not able to go to university, as I wanted to do. I couldn't understand why I failed my 'A' levels because I got really good grades in my 'O' level examinations (Ordinary Level). I joined a one-year Travel and Tourism course because I loved languages and the thought of traveling as well. I failed that too. It was soon after this that I went to work for the large local authority. Over a period of the next twenty years, whilst at work, not only did I gain qualifications equivalent to Advanced Level and which were also work-related, I had also gained my degree in psychology. The result was that my workplace paid for my education, and I gladly accepted.

I always believed in having a good education, even from an early age, so the fact that I didn't get the required qualifications earlier on, motivated me over the years to acquire these. As I write this book, I am taking a break from academic studying before embarking on further studies to expand on my expertise.

The bottom line is, I love to study. Looking back on my childhood days, I probably used studying as a form of escape from a dysfunctional family setting, whereas now, I am conscious that I study because I thoroughly enjoy it and see it as part and parcel of my ongoing personal and professional development. To this day, education is a strong theme in our household and I strive to ensure that my children get the best education possible.

You can use negative experiences in your own life, as well as harnessing the positive images of your achievements and successes.

To keep myself focused on the future I have a strong vision of the house I want to live in. I can see this beautiful building, set in a lovely garden and overlooking a river. I know the exact layout of the garden and where each flower will go. I can walk through the front door and I know exactly what the entrance hall and staircase looks like. I've added features and facilities as I decide what I want. I've bought place mats with images that remind me of my dream house. I have these in my current home to inspire me.

I talk about my future home, I write about it in my journal and I think about it with passion. This underpins all my actions that will achieve the success that I need in order to buy this beautiful home. Whilst I am not necessarily a materialistic person, my dream house is one of the visions I use to propel me to my future success.

A vision this powerful will overcome any blips that may occur in my journey to success.

What's your vision that draws you on?

Welcome the challenges that occur for they are what make you grow if you take time to learn from them and take action to make changes.

Live your dream. You only have one life to live and when it is gone, it is gone. Make the most of the time you have here and now. Think of the legacy you will leave your children or other members of your family

What are the things in your life that motivate you today? What are the negative things that occurred in your life that are your driving force for you to achieve your goals today?

Is it failed education?

Childhood issues?

Lack of promotion at work?

Rejection?

Whatever the reasons, these are called 'Away from Motivation' goals, because you are moving away from the negative experiences in your life and using them to drive you forward, for example, my education. You are moving away from these experiences because you never want to repeat them again.

Alternatively, what are the positive things in your life that you want to achieve in the future that are your driving force?

Is it a buying a particular house?

A particular business?

Helping others..?

Family values and vision?

Financial goals?

Spiritual goals?

These are called 'Towards Motivation' goals. You have a vision of something you want to achieve in the future and you strive to achieve it, my house for example.

Find out what motivates you and stick with it.

"Use your precious moments to live life fully every single second of every single day."
Marcia Wieder

Lose Excess Baggage

If you want to fly and really be successful you need to lose any excess baggage you are carrying right now. Excess baggage only serves to weigh you down.

By excess baggage I mean negative people in your life, including family, friends and associates.

I have a cousin who is very thoughtful and helpful; however, she is also very negative. She is in a very dysfunctional relationship and whenever we meet, she always wants to tell me about the situation with her partner. After a while, each time she started talking about him, I would attempt to cut the conversation short by reminding her "You always knew what he was like. You are just as responsible, what are you going to do about it?"

Now when she starts on the topic I either make a quick exit for the door or don't respond to any of her comments on this subject. Now she rarely talks about him to me as much as she used to and I have reduced my contacts with her. I see her less and less these days, though she is still there in the frame as part of my extended family.

This is not an easy thing to do, but it is necessary. Some negative people around you will naturally fall by the wayside anyway as they see you grow. Some will try to keep you back. Decide what is best for you.

This may seem a little harsh; however, it is a reality of life that we need to make choices and not all of our choices and decisions will be easy. All successful entrepreneurs need to make decisions. This will be one of those that will put you to the test.

I am still single nine years after my divorce, not because I haven't had offers of marriage along the way, but because I haven't yet met anyone who I feel is going in my direction, who is able to lead me or at least be able to keep up with me. They've got to be able to live with a Winner!

What I do have though is clear focus and a very clear idea of the kind of partner and husband that I want to attract and have in my life. Having the wrong partner in my life right now for the sake of having a partner is an unnecessary stress, burden and more baggage than I can afford.

Attitude

"It is our own mental attitude which makes the world what it is for us. Our thought makes things beautiful, our thoughts make things ugly. The whole world is in our own minds."
Swami Vivekananda

Attitude is everything. Have a positive, 'can do' attitude. Catch yourself speaking negatively of yourself and others and interrupt this pattern by using positive affirmations. I have embraced the saying that goes 'if you don't have anything good to say then don't say anything at all.'

Recently I enquired about a new business account and the Business Manager at the new bank asked me what my existing bank was like as she had heard some 'awful' things about them. My response was "Business is business. Even if they were the worst business bankers, I still wouldn't say."

That stopped the discussion going down a negative path and we were able to get back on track with her providing me with relevant information I needed in order to make an informed decision about moving my business account. The rapport between us was even better than when we first started the meeting.

> *"Attitudes are far more important than facts."*
> *Dr Karl Menninger*

Act As If

Another of the secrets of great achievers is that they act as if they are already a great achiever. Their focus is definitely on the end result. Try it and see the benefits for yourself.

Perseverance

If you have a situation that you are dealing with and feel like giving up, dig your heels in and keep going. There is always a solution to any given situation that you are faced with.

As I said earlier, the fact that I didn't know what to do as a new business start up was not an excuse for me not to start my business or to give up. I had self-belief that I would find the answer and that I was meant to be in business and be successful. Although my initial couple of years were not that successful, this experience did not deter me from persevering and to find 'me' within the business world.

I had experienced trial and error, failures and getting stuck on a plateau. I had experienced people looking at me as if to say 'She doesn't know what she is doing'. At one stage I even told myself 'I don't know what I am doing.' However, I never thought for one moment that I would give up. That is not what my journey is about. I've always been 100% focused on success. I have had to have lots of sheer perseverance and determination to arrive at this stage. Now I have found my niche market which has enabled everything else to fall into place.

So even when things seem at their worst, this is when you need to dig your heels in one more time to find the answer to your challenges.   Where there is a will there is a way! Ask powerful questions of your mentor and everyone who may be able to support you with your situation.

Jordan Productions research shows that over 80% of small businesses fail in the first two years. The Department of Trade and Industry has similar statistics.

Will you be one of the statistics or will you do whatever necessary to become the success you deserve to be?

"History has demonstrated that the most notable winners usually encountered heartbreaking obstacles before they triumphed. They won because they refused to become discouraged by their defeats."
Bertie C. Forbes

In terms of the transition from personal development to business development, below are just a few areas of business development that, if you were to transfer your personal development and learning to them, will make a great deal of difference for you and your customers.

Implementing the business development strategies below will also be a testament of your journey and a testament of your own self-belief in your service or products.

Long Term Relationship With Clients

The aim of interacting with prospective customers is to convert them into long term paying clients. This is done through repeat business. Most important however, is how you treat your customer in order for this to happen. Treat people how you would want to be treated.

Do unto others as you would have them do unto you.

Think of a service or product that you just bought recently, however, the people service was not very good.

How would you have done it differently?

What would have made that service better for you?

Whatever your answers, approach your own customers in the same vain.

Stay in touch with them.

Be their best friend.

Develop trust over time.

Again, and most importantly, develop YOU first.

Risk Reversal

I offer a 100% money back guarantee on all my training courses and seminars. This is simply another way of adding value to your customers. It shows your prospective client that you are so sure of the benefits of your product or service that you are willing to put your money where your mouth is!

From the customer's point of view, they are a winner whatever they decide to do. This creates a win-win situation between you and your customers or clients, which builds the customer's trust and confidence in you and your products or service.

If you offer a money back guarantee you must honour it. Always keep your word to your customers - bad news travels fast and you can't afford people to talk about you in a negative way!

I will always remember the unfortunate experience I had with the business coach who did not honour his money back guarantee. After the first session with him,

I decided that his approach was not for me and asked for my money back. To my surprise (given where I had met him) he said that the money back guarantee is only valid if his coaching did not work. Opting out of the process in my books means that his coaching did not work.

When you love what you do, develop the confidence and belief in what you do, then you will be in a position to offer your customers this benefit.

Referrals

The aim of being in business is for your business to grow and develop. Getting referrals plays a big part in this.

Customise your service or product so that new and existing customers know you operate on a referral basis. The benefit of this is that by having prospective customers referred to you, they are already 'warm' and are aware of who you are and what you offer.

Most satisfied customers are more than happy to give you referrals, but may not think about it without some prompting. Perhaps you could build in a reward for your customer for the referral.

Products

Have products available as back end sales for your customers and clients. This has numerous implications:

It helps with your repeat business;

It improves your profits;

Your clients become long-term clients (if you treat them right);

You appear as an expert in your field of business, gaining celebrity status and clearly raising your profile simultaneously.

What's even smarter is if you bundle your products and sell them as a special offer to increase more sales.

If you are selling services, selling products also is a quicker way of getting into the international market place.

Work On Your Business

Making time to work 'on' your business and not just in it is absolutely crucial if you want it to succeed. This gets you focused on developing all other aspects of the business rather than just being a technician within it.

I have decided that working 'on' my business Saturday morning is the best day for me at the moment. I am working on my business during the week on an ongoing basis, but Saturday morning is my main thinking and planning time. I seize the opportunity to work on the business for a couple of hours before I take my son to football.

Michael Gerber's E-Myth Revisited is an excellent book written especially for small businesses. It explains the process of developing your business in great detail. What I learnt most was about the need to have systems in your business which would enable your business to run without you being physically present. My other learning point was that people buy what they want and not what they need. This has helped me to rethink my marketing.

Having worked on the business, I felt the paradigm shift in moving from being self-employed to becoming a business owner. They are most certainly on two different spheres and simply do not compare.

How You Can Use This Chapter For Winning Success:

- Decide on your plan to move yourself forward and take action.

- Decide what you will use to motivate you when the going gets tough and stick to it.

- Identify your life plan. What is your life vision?

- Find at least one role model or mentor that you can work with and that you trust.

- Make time to work 'on' your business.

- Get your attitude right if it needs attention

- Do what you love to do

How Jennifer McLeod Can Help You Further

FREE Inspirational monthly newsletter via email (ezine)

Open Seminars and Training Courses

Retreats

Inspirational Relationship and Divorce Coaching

Speaking Engagements

Consultancy Services

www.PositiveInspirationS.co.uk

Share Your Success Story

We want to hear your success story.

Tell us how our books, courses, seminars and audio programmes have helped you. What difference have they made to your life and or business?

Inspire other entrepreneurs into action. It may just be that hearing about your success is exactly what someone else needs to give them the motivation they need.

Send us a short summary, no more than 500 words, and we will do our best to publicise your achievements in our future products or seminars. This will help to raise your profile and give you the recognition that you deserve.

We look forward to hearing from you.

Send your summary to us via our website: www.PositiveInspirationS.co.uk or to:

Step Up! International Ltd

Inspirational House

Friary Rd

Handsworth Wood

Birmingham

England

B20 1BB